THE GO-AHEAD MAN

THE GO-AHEAD MAN

TYRONE JOHNSON

authorHOUSE®

AuthorHouse™
1663 Liberty Drive
Bloomington, IN 47403
www.authorhouse.com
Phone: 1 (800) 839-8640

Published by AuthorHouse 04/21/2015

ISBN: 978-1-5049-0869-6 (sc)
ISBN: 978-1-5049-0870-2 (hc)
ISBN: 978-1-5049-0868-9 (e)

Library of Congress Control Number: 2015906318

CONTENTS

DEDICATION

This book is dedicated to my wife Diane, who believed in and encouraged me every step of the way. Diane, I love you, and I know you will be patient with me as I struggle to be your go-ahead man. Thank you, Darling you are special to me and I will always love you.

INTRODUCTION

Luke 23:34 *Then said Jesus, Father, forgive them; for they know not what they do. And they parted his raiment, and cast lots.*

John 15:13-15 *Greater love hath no man than this, that a man lay down his life for his friends14 Ye are my friends, if ye do whatsoever I command you.15 Henceforth I call you not servants; for the servant knoweth not what his lord doeth: but I have called you friends; for all things that I have heard of my Father I have made known unto you.*

In Luke 23:34, Jesus shows us how to get along with our enemies, and in John 15:13-15, Jesus shows us how to get alone with our friends. But how do we get along with our spouses? Jesus didn't leave us an example of that. Or did He? In Eph.5:22-32, Paul compares Christ's relationship to the church to the relationship of the husband and the wife. In Paul's comparison he makes mention of a great mystery, in which he refers to the working together of the members of our body, Paul also calls Christ's relationship to the church a great mystery. While praying about writing this book, the Holy Spirit showed me that most Christians experience their greatest battle from the enemy while in their own homes. This attack from the enemy usually comes through the husband or the wife. Unlike most problems that are solved by going the root of the problem, this problem is solved by going to the head. "The man is the head of the wife" is a quote right out of the Bible, and if misunderstood, will do the marriage more harm than good.

The Go-Ahead Man is written to give the reader an easy to understand guide to strengthening their marriage through sacrifice and servant hood. Every husband has the ability to be a go-ahead man.; all he needs is himself. Just like Christ gave Himself for the church, the go-ahead man gives himself for the marriage. The most valuable thing that anyone can give to someone is themselves.

Chapter I

I Am Somebody

The Declaration of Independence of 1776 states, "*We hold these truths to be self-evident, that all men are created equal, that they are endowed by their Creator with certain unalienable Rights, that among these are Life, Liberty and the pursuit of Happiness.*" The Declaration of Independence is a good thing, and it also agrees with what the Word of God teaches. The term "self-evident" means "*evident in itself without proof or demonstration.*" The Declaration of Independence is saying that this truth is obvious and should go without saying. Nevertheless, the writers of this document took the time to put it in writing so there would be no misunderstanding.

We can also see self-evident truths in the Word of God. These truths should also be obvious and go without saying, but God took the time to put them in writing so that there would be no misunderstanding. The idea from the Declaration of Independence that "*all men are created equal*" came from the Word of God and is a goal mankind should reach for. In God's eyes, we were all created equal. I thank God that He does not categorize people the way we do. God only sees us in two categories: have you accepted his son Jesus or not?

The Bible teaches us that there is no respect of persons with God. He shows no partiality and looks at all his covenant children the same.

1 Peter 1:17 *And if ye call on the Father, who without respect of persons judgeth according to every man's work, pass the time of your sojourning here in fear.*

Col 3:25 *But he that doeth wrong shall receive for the wrong which he hath done: and there is no respect of persons*

Eph 6:9 *And, ye masters, do the same things unto them, forbearing threatening: knowing that your Master also is in heaven; neither is there respect of persons with him.*

As the Holy Spirit teaches us that there is no respect of persons with God, the Spirit also teaches us that we have a responsibility to God and to His Word. When I finally realized this truth, I asked myself, "If there is no respect of persons with God, who or what determines my lot in life?" I began to understand that while there may not be a respect of persons with God, there is a respect of purpose. I realized how important it is that I discover my purpose and walk in it. The main struggle we will have with the enemy is that he will try to keep us from discovering our purpose, as he seeks to steal our destiny. Satan knows that when we find out why we are on this earth he will never be able to stop us. Jesus teaches us this in John 10:10

John 10:10 *The thief cometh not, but for to steal, and to kill, and to destroy: I am come that they might have life, and that they might have it more abundantly.*

We learn from John 10:10 that Jesus didn't just come to give us life but to give us abundant life and we will not have abundant life in the earth if we are not living out our purpose.

What on Earth Am I Here For

Every believer should understand that God wants us to be happy, and as we allow God to lead us in every area of our lives, He gives us joy and also makes us free. As God's created beings, God knows that we will never have joy if we are bound so He makes us free. God gives us free will, which also allows us to sin against Him, but He knows if He is to experience true love from us He must first let us go. Being free, I believe, is what every person desires; some of us are just not aware of it yet. Most people do not realize what true freedom is all about. We can only be free if Christ makes us free. Being free means *"free to do as one pleases or desires."* Our true desires come from our creator, and these desires that we get from our creator do not include sin. In order for us to walk in our desires we must go through our creator. This is why Jesus said in John 8:36

John 8:36 *If the Son therefore shall make you free, ye shall be free indeed.*

Jesus is the only one who can truly make us free. Even as Christ has made us free, He has also made us free to choose whether we want to walk in that freedom or not. God is not going to make us do the right thing we can make bad choices every day and all day lone God will not stop us. One thing that I have come to realize as I have gotten older is that true happiness only comes when we are doing what God created us to do.

Home Sweet Home?

While I was praying about this book, God asked me, "Tyrone, where do you think most Christians experience their greatest defeat?" It didn't take me long to come up with the answer, and I said, "In the home." And God said, "Yes, that's right, in the home." I began to think about the old sayings, "A man's home is his castle," and "Home is where the heart is." Those sayings hold some truth, but there is something else that happens in the home: the enemy attacks. Our homes are where the enemy works the hardest to get us out of fellowship with God. The next question I asked God was, "How can we overcome in this struggle?"

I was amazed when God said, "to solve most problems, you must go to the root of the problem and destroy it from the root, but to solve this problem you must go to the head." What God meant by this is that we must look to the head of the household, the man, because the man is not just the head of the problem he is also part of the root of the problem.

"The man is the head of the woman", what does it really mean? That is another question I asked God, and He replied, "It means the man is to go ahead."

Eph 5:23 For the husband is the head of the wife, even as Christ is the head of the church: and he is the saviour of the body.

Religions have long misunderstood what headship or leadership means. We have been taught that it means being in charge or being the boss, telling others what to do. But that is the world's definitions of headship. God's definition of headship is the opposite of the world's definition; to God it means being a servant.

Matt 20:26-27 But it shall not be so among you: but whosoever will be great among you, let him be your minister; 27 And whosoever will be chief among you, let him be your servant.

Christ's Bride

Being a go-ahead husband means being a servant, going ahead and setting the pace, making the way clear, being an example. In other words, it means being like Jesus. Jesus has shown us how to live by leaving us examples. One might say, "Jesus was never married so He doesn't understand what I am going through with this woman." Oh, but Christ is married to the church. The Holy Spirit gives us a great example in Eph 5:25-32.

Eph 5:25-32 Husbands, love your wives, even as Christ also loved the church, and gave himself for it; 26 That he might sanctify and cleanse it with the washing of water by the word, 27 That he might present it to himself a glorious church, not having spot, or wrinkle, or any such thing; but that it should be holy and without blemish. 28 So ought men to love their wives as their own bodies. He that loveth his wife loveth himself. 29 For no man ever yet hated his own flesh; but nourisheth and cherisheth it, even as the

5

Lord the church: 30 For we are members of his body, of his flesh, and of his bones. 31 For this cause shall a man leave his father and mother, and shall be joined unto his wife, and they two shall be one flesh. 32 This is a great mystery: but I speak concerning Christ and the church.

The Holy Spirit parallels the relationship of Christ and the church to the relationship of the husband and the wife. When we look closely at Christ's relationship to the church in this passage, we see that Christ shows us exactly what our roles are as husbands. Paul calls this relationship "a great mystery."

Seeing what Jesus does for the church and the plans He has for the church shows us how the go-ahead man should treat his wife and the plans he should have for his family. Husbands, God have given us the go-ahead. He has gone ahead of us and made the way for us. God has made it possible for us to be go-ahead men. So go ahead, husbands. Take the head and lead your family into a life of liberty and into a pursuit of happiness and prosperity.

Scriptures Chapter I

Luke 23:34 *Then said Jesus, Father, forgive them; for they know not what they do. And they parted his raiment, and cast lots.*

John 15:13-15 *Greater love hath no man than this, that a man lay down his life for his friends14 Ye are my friends, if ye do whatsoever I command you.15 Henceforth I call you not servants; for the servant knoweth not what his lord doeth: but I have called you friends; for all things that I have heard of my Father I have made known unto you.*

1 Peter 1:17 *And if ye call on the Father, who without respect of persons judgeth according to every man's work, pass the time of your sojourning here in fear.*

Col 3:25 *But he that doeth wrong shall receive for the wrong which he hath done: and there is no respect of persons.*

Eph 6:9 *And, ye masters, do the same things unto them, forbearing threatening: knowing that your Master also is in heaven; neither is there respect of persons with him.*

John 10:10 *The thief cometh not, but for to steal, and to kill, and to destroy: I am come that they might have life, and that they might have it more abundantly.*

John 8:36 *If the Son therefore shall make you free, ye shall be free indeed.*

Eph 5:23 *For the husband is the head of the wife, even as Christ is the head of the church: and he is the saviour of the body.*

Matt 20:26-27 *But it shall not be so among you: but whosoever will be great among you, let him be your minister; 27 And whosoever will be chief among you, let him be your servant.*

Eph 5:25-32 *Husbands, love your wives, even as Christ also loved the church, and gave himself for it;26 That he might sanctify and cleanse it with the washing of water by the word,27 That he might present it to himself a glorious church, not having spot, or wrinkle, or any such thing; but that it should be holy and without blemish.28 So ought men to love their wives as their own bodies. He that loveth his wife loveth himself.29 For no man ever yet hated his own flesh, but nourisheth and cherisheth it, even as the Lord the church:30 For we are members of his body, of his flesh, and of his bones.31 For this cause shall a man leave his father and mother, and shall be joined unto his wife, and they two shall be one flesh.32 This is a great mystery: but I speak concerning Christ and the church.*

CHAPTER II

THE GREAT MYSTERY

What is a mystery? A mystery is something hidden, or covered, a secret. For our purposes, we will say a mystery is a hidden truth. Some mysteries are not true, but since we are talking about the Word of God, we can use the word "truth." The word mystery comes from the Greek word "μυστήριον" pronounced *musteérion*, meaning "*a secret*." I enjoy watching a good mystery on TV, or reading a good mystery novel, but to truly enjoy a good mystery, at some point we must be able to understand the mystery. It would do us very little good to study the mysteries of the Bible without ever understanding them. When a mystery is revealed, it is no longer a mystery; it then becomes a revelation.

In my studies of theology, I find it very interesting that the word revelation does not appear in the Old Testament (KJV) at all, but the word "secret" appears fifty-two times. As we study the Old Testament books, we find that they are full of excitement and adventures; it is somewhat like reading a mystery novel or a thrilling adventure. As we study these books, we can't help but ask questions and wonder why. Why did God do things the way He did? Why did God tell Abraham to sacrifice his son Isaac? God must have known that Abraham would obey Him, and I am sure that God also knew that He would stop Abraham and not allow him the kill his son. Why did God smite Egypt ten times before Pharaoh would let the people go? Surely God could have made Pharaoh release the children of Israel after just one smite or even no smiting at all. Fifteen times in the book of Exodus, the Bible says that Pharaoh's heart was hardened, but five of those times the Bible says the Lord hardened Pharaoh's heart. Doesn't that make you wonder? Why would God harden Pharaoh's heart, and then smite him for having a hard heart? The Old Testament is full of mysteries and reasons to ask, "Why?" Just like the Old Testament is full of mysteries, the New Testament is full of revelations.

Revelation

The word revelation means *"an uncovering, something revealed."* While this definition of revelation is accurate, it is somewhat incomplete. Revelation is an uncovering or something revealed, but for revelation to benefit us, revelation must be received.

John 3:27 John answered and said, A man can receive nothing, except it be given him from heaven.

Revelation comes in different degrees to different people. Two people can go to the same church and hear the same sermon; one will get the revelation and the other may not. I was in church for years before I got the revelation that God really does love me and actually cares about the little things in my life. During all that time, the Word of God did not change. God's Word kept saying the same thing, but I had to change the way I was thinking about the Word of God and receive what God had been saying all along. Revelation must be sought after and received; in fact, anything that you get from God must be sought after and received.

Prov 25:2 *It is the glory of God to conceal a thing: but the honour of kings is to search out a matter.*

Most revelations, when received, look so simple it makes you want to say, "Why didn't I see that sooner?" Most of the mysteries of the Old Testament are not mysteries to us because we have read the end of the book, and God has uncovered the mystery for us in the New Testament.

As I studied the Old Testament prophecies of the Bible, I could see that at the time they were spoken, they were mysteries. But now that we have the New Testament Scriptures, what was a mystery in the Old Testament is now revealed as revelation in the New Testament.

The Mystery of the Church

One of the greatest mysteries of the Bible is the church. The mystery of the church is so complex that at first glance it doesn't even appear to be there. Have you ever wondered what Jesus meant when He said in Matt. 16:18

Matt 16:18 *And I say also unto thee, That thou art Peter, and upon this rock I will build my church; and the gates of hell shall not prevail against it.*

I used to think that Matt 16:18 meant that if I went to church then I would not have hell in my life, but I soon found out that this is not true. As I began to study Matt 16:18, I found some very interesting things about the church: the church has a foundation, the church is supposed to stand, the church belongs to Christ, the church builder is Christ, opposition will arise against Christ's church, and the church will prevail in the end. As we understand these things about the church, we understand more about the church and its purpose. The word church in the Greek is pronounced *"ek-klay-see'-ah"* meaning *"a calling out, to invite, to name, to call."* From this definition, one of the most important things I realized about the church is that the church is holy, meaning *"set apart for God, to be, as it were, exclusively his, one mind with God."* When we look at these characteristics about the church, we quickly realize that the church is not the building, neither is the church any certain denomination, race, nationality, entity, or religious group. The church is made up of those who have answered the invitation of Christ to come out of a lifestyle of sin.

John 6:44 *No man can come to me, except the Father, which hath sent me, draw him: and I will raise him up at the last day.*

Rev 3:20 *Behold, I stand at the door, and knock: if any man hear my voice, and open the door, I will come in to him, and will sup with him, and he with me.*

God often uses parables about one thing to teach us something totally different. The Holy Spirit uses Paul in Eph 5:22-33 to show the parallel between Christ and the church and the husband and the wife.

Eph 5:22-33 *Wives, submit yourselves unto your own husbands, as unto the Lord.*

23 For the husband is the head of the wife, even as Christ is the head of the church: and he is the saviour of the body.24 Therefore as the church is subject unto Christ, so let the wives be to their own husbands in every thing.25 Husbands, love your wives, even as Christ also loved the church, and gave himself for it;26 That he might sanctify and cleanse it with the washing of water by the word,27 That he might present it to himself a glorious church, not having spot, or wrinkle, or any such thing; but that it should be holy and without blemish.28 So ought men to love their wives as their own bodies. He that loveth his wife loveth himself.29 For no man ever yet hated his own flesh; but nourisheth and cherisheth it, even as the Lord the church:30 For we are members of his body, of his flesh, and of his bones.31 For this cause shall a man leave his father and mother, and shall be joined unto his wife, and they two shall be one flesh.32 This is a great mystery: but I speak concerning Christ and the church.33 Nevertheless let every one of you in particular so love his wife even as himself; and the wife see that she reverence her husband.

In Eph 5:32, Paul calls this a mystery, and through this mystery, the Holy Spirit teaches men how to treat their wives and wives how to respond to their husbands. One might say, "Why Eph 5:22-33"? I believe it is because this Scripture shows the unconditional love Christ has for His church.

Unconditional love means love without conditions; not "I love you because," but just "I love you," period. The problem with "I love you because" is that if the "because" changes then the love changes, and that means you have love with conditions.

We can easily understand conditional love. If you love me, then I will love you. The big problem with conditional love is that with conditions come expectations. When expectations are not met, there are disappointments. Disappointments can lead to arguments and arguments can lead to divorce. See the progression?

Let's look at this great mystery that Paul is speaking about. To truly understand this mystery, as with anything else in the Bible, we must go back to the beginning, the book of Genesis. When God created the world, He did it by speaking Words.

John 1:1-3 *In the beginning was the Word, and the Word was with God, and the Word was God. 2 The same was in the beginning with God. 3 All things were made by him; and without him was not any thing made that was made.*

When God got ready to create the plants, He spoke to the ground. When He got ready to create the stars, He spoke to the firmament. But when He got ready to created man, He spoke to Himself.

Gen 2:7 *And the Lord God formed man of the dust of the ground, and breathed into his nostrils the breath of life; and man became a living soul.*

God had fellowship with Adam and Eve in the garden. They had come to look forward to God walking with them in the cool of the day. I believe that God enjoyed being with them; after all, they were made in His image and in His likeness. When God looked at Adam, it was like looking in a mirror. Man was just like God and man was one with God. In other words, man had it going on. WOW.

Gen 3:8 *And they heard the voice of the Lord God walking in the garden in the cool of the day.*

Life in the Garden

Man had a one-on-one relationship with God, but when man sinned, it brought division between God and man. Man experienced instant spiritual death and was separated from God. Can you imagine how God must have felt when His wonderful creation was lost? After all, God had high hopes and big plans for man. God created man to live forever. Man was never meant to die, but with sin comes death.

Rom 6:23 *For the wages of sin is death; but the gift of God is eternal life through Jesus Christ our Lord.*

God did not and would not give up on man. God had a plan that would put Him back in relationship with man. But in order for God to put His plan into action, He needed a man. You might wonder, since God is almighty why does He need a man. The Bible explains:

Gen 1:26 *And God said, Let us make man in our image, after our likeness: and let them have dominion over the fish of the sea, and over the fowl of the air, and over the cattle, and over all the earth, and over every creeping thing that creepeth upon the earth.*

We see in Gen. 1:26 that God has given man dominion on earth. Since God has spoken, He cannot go back on His word. And since man has dominion, man has to be part of God's plan.

1 Peter 1:18-20 Forasmuch as ye know that ye were not redeemed with corruptible things, as silver and gold, from your vain conversation received by tradition from your fathers; 19 But with the precious blood of Christ, as of a lamb without blemish and without spot: 20 Who verily was foreordained before the foundation of the world, but was manifest in these last times for you.

God foreknew man's fall before He created the earth, so He had a plan for man. 1 Peter 1:18-20 declares that God had a plan before the foundations of the world. For the sake of our understanding, the Bible tells us about the search for someone to redeem man.

Rev 5:1-5 And I saw in the right hand of him that sat on the throne a book written within and on the backside, sealed with seven seals. 2 And I saw a strong angel proclaiming with a loud voice, Who is worthy to open the book, and to loose the seals thereof? 3 And no man in heaven, nor in earth, neither under the earth, was able to open the book, neither to look thereon. 4 And I wept much, because no man was found worthy to open and to read the book, neither to look thereon.

5 And one of the elders saith unto me, Weep not: behold, the Lion of the tribe of Judah, the Root of David, hath prevailed to open the book, and to loose the seven seals thereof.

No one was found, but God created a man's body and placed Himself in it and became our savior. We know this man as Jesus. (WOW, GOD IS AWESOME.)

God to the Rescue!

God's main desire was to get back the fellowship He once had with man, the relationship that He had with Adam in the garden. God began to put the plan in motion:

1 Peter 1:20 who verily was foreordained before the foundation of the world, but was manifest in these last times for you.

The purpose of God's plan was to get man back to Himself, which we now know as the plan of salvation, or *"σωζω,"* pronounced *"sozo"* and meaning *"be made whole."* Man had lost something in the garden and Jesus gave man the opportunity to get it back. Man made a choice in the garden and chose to disobey God and obey Satan. So God gave man the opportunity to make another choice, to obey Him. God knows that not all men will come back to Him, but He calls all men to Himself.

Revelation 3:20 Behold, I stand at the door and knock. If any man hears my voice and open the door I will come in to him, and will sup with him and he with me.

God's First Church Members

We get the word church from *"ek-klay-see'-ah,"* "a calling out." God calls us out and when we answer Him, we become part of His church. We began to read about the church in the New Testament but, actually, references are made to the church throughout the Bible, beginning with Noah. When God told Noah to build an ark because it was going to rain, it had never rained on earth before, so that was a mystery to Noah. Noah's obedience to God was totally an act of faith; this is why Noah is mentioned in what is known as: *The Hall of Fame of faith.*

Heb 11:7 By faith, Noah, being warned of God of things not seen as yet, moved with fear, prepared an ark to the saving of his house; by the which he condemned the world, and became heir of the righteousness which is by faith.

Because of Noah's actions of faith, God makes a covenant with Noah:

Gen 9:9 And I, behold, I establish my covenant with you, and with your seed after you;

Abraham, who was a great-great-grandson of Noah, was also *"ek-klay-see'-ah,"* or you could say called out by God

Gen 17:19 And God said, Sarah, your wife, shall bear you a son indeed: and you shall call his name Isaac: and I will establish My covenant with him for an everlasting Covenant and with his seed after him.

We can clearly see that the church was on the mind of God from the very beginning. God has always had great plans for His *called out ones* and because man has dominion on earth, God's plans had to go through man. God needed to find a man that believed Him, and He found Noah and then Abraham.

Gen 15:6 *And he (Abraham) believed in the LORD; and he counted it to him for righteousness.*

Because Abraham believed God, God made him righteous. But what did God tell Abraham so that he could believe; God preached the Gospel to Abraham and Abraham believed it.

Gal 3:8-9 *And the scripture, foreseeing that God would justify the heathen through faith, preached before the gospel unto Abraham, saying, In thee shall all nations be blessed. ⁹So then they which be of faith are blessed with faithful Abraham.*

So from this we can understand that to be part of the church, a called out one, we must believe the gospel and the gospel is, "we are blessed because our sins are forgiven." When we believe the gospel, we are made righteous just like Abraham were made righteous. When we believe we are righteous, we will begin to do the right things. Note what the Holy Spirit says in Romans *1: 16-17:*

Rom 1:16-17 *For I am not ashamed of the gospel of Christ: for it is the power of God unto salvation to every one that believeth; to the Jew first, and also* *to the Greek.* *¹⁷* *For therein is the righteousness of God revealed from faith to faith: as it is written, The just shall live by faith.*

Since we are Abraham's seed, through Christ, that means we are part of the family!

Gen 18:18 *since his family will become a great and powerful nation that will be a blessing to all other nations on earth.*

Again, God says to Abraham:

Gen 22:18 *you have obeyed me, and so you and your descendants will be a blessing to all nations on earth."*

Gen 17:7 *I will always keep the promise I have made to you and your descendants, because I am your God and their God.*

On the day of Pentecost, when Peter and the others were in the upper room, the Holy Ghost began to reveal to Peter the mind of God concerning the church.

Acts 3:22-25 *Moses said, "The Lord your God will choose one of your own people to be a prophet, just as he chose me. Listen to everything he tells you.* *²³* *No one who disobeys that prophet will be one of God's people any longer."*²⁴ *Samuel and all the other prophets who came later also spoke about what is now happening.* *²⁵* *You are really the ones God told his prophets to speak to. And you were given the promise that God made to* *your ancestors. He said to Abraham, "All nations on earth will be blessed because of someone from your family."*

Gal 3:29 *And if you be in Christ's then are you Abraham's seed, and heirs according to the promise.*

So the mystery began to come to light, and it is no longer a mystery it is a revelation. I am sure Peter must have thought, "Why didn't I see that sooner?"

SCRIPTURES CHAPTER II

John 3:27 *John answered and said, A man can receive nothing, except it be given him from heaven.*

Prov 25:2 *It is the glory of God to conceal a thing: but the honour of kings is to search out a matter.*

Matt 16:18 *And I say also unto thee, That thou art Peter, and upon this rock I will build my church; and the gates of hell shall not prevail against it.*

John 6:44 *No man can come to me, except the Father which hath sent me draw him: and I will raise him up at the last day.*

Rev 3:20 *Behold, I stand at the door, and knock: if any man hear my voice, and open the door, I will come in to him, and will sup with him, and he with me.*

Eph 5:22-33 *Wives, submit yourselves unto your own husbands, as unto the Lord.23 For the husband is the head of the wife, even as Christ is the head of the church: and he is the saviour of the body.24 Therefore as the church is subject unto Christ, so let the wives be to their own husbands in every thing.25 Husbands, love your wives, even as Christ also loved the church, and gave himself for it;26 That he might sanctify and cleanse it with the washing of water by the word,27 That he might present it to himself a glorious church, not having spot, or wrinkle, or any such thing; but that it should be holy and without blemish.28 So ought men to love their wives as their own bodies. He that loveth his wife loveth himself.29 For no man ever yet hated his own flesh; but nourisheth and cherisheth it, even as the Lord the church:30 For we are members of his body, of his flesh, and of his bones.31 For this cause shall a man leave his father and mother, and shall be joined unto his wife, and they two shall be one flesh.32 This is a great mystery: but I speak concerning Christ and the church.33 Nevertheless let every one of you in particular so love his wife even as himself; and the wife see that she reverence her husband.*

John 1:1-3 *In the beginning was the Word, and the Word was with God, and the Word was God.2 The same was in the beginning with God.3 All things were made by him; and without him was not any thing made that was made.*

Gen 2:7 *And the Lord God formed man of the dust of the ground, and breathed into his nostrils the breath of life; and man became a living soul.*

Gen 3:8 *And they heard the voice of the Lord God walking in the garden in the cool of the day: and Adam and his wife hid themselves from the presence of the Lord God amongst the trees of the garden.*

Rom 6:23 *For the wages of sin is death; but the gift of God is eternal life through Jesus Christ our Lord.*

Gen 1:26 *And God said, Let us make man in our image, after our likeness: and let them have dominion over the fish of the sea, and over the fowl of the air, and over the cattle, and over all the earth, and over every creeping thing that creepeth upon the earth.*

1 Peter 1:18-20 *Forasmuch as ye know that ye were not redeemed with corruptible things, as silver and gold, from your vain conversation received by tradition from your fathers;19 But with the precious blood of Christ, as of a lamb without blemish and without spot:20 Who verily was foreordained before the foundation of the world, but was manifest in these last times for you.*

Rev 5:1-5 *And I saw in the right hand of him that sat on the throne a book written within and on the backside, sealed with seven seals.2 And I saw a strong angel proclaiming with a loud voice, Who is worthy to open the book, and to loose the seals thereof?3 And no man in heaven, nor in earth, neither under the earth, was able to open the book, neither to look thereon.4 And I wept much, because no man was found worthy to open and to read the book, neither to look thereon.5 And one of the elders saith unto me, Weep not: behold, the Lion of the tribe of Judah, the Root of David, hath prevailed to open the book, and to loose the seven seals thereof.*

1 Peter 1:20 *Who verily was foreordained before the foundation of the world, but was manifest in these last times for you.*

Rev 3:20 *Behold, I stand at the door, and knock: if any man hear my voice, and open the door, I will come in to him, and will sup with him, and he with me.*

Heb 11:7 *By faith Noah, being warned of God of things not seen as yet, moved with fear, prepared an ark to the saving of his house; by the which he condemned the world, and became heir of the righteousness which is by faith.*

Gen 9:9 *And I, behold, I establish my covenant with you, and with your seed after you.*

Gen 17:19 *And God said, Sarah thy wife shall bear thee a son indeed; and thou shalt call his name Isaac: and I will establish my covenant with him for an everlasting covenant, and with his seed after him.*

Gen 15:6 *And he believed in the Lord; and he counted it to him for righteousness.*

Gal 3:8-9 *And the scripture, foreseeing that God would justify the heathen through faith, preached before the gospel unto Abraham, saying, In thee shall all nations be blessed.9 So then they which be of faith are blessed with faithful Abraham.*

Rom 1:16-17 *For I am not ashamed of the gospel of Christ: for it is the power of God unto salvation to every one that believeth; to the Jew first, and also to the Greek.17*

For therein is the righteousness of God revealed from faith to faith: as it is written, The just shall live by faith.

Gen 18:18 *Seeing that Abraham shall surely become a great and mighty nation, and all the nations of the earth shall be blessed in him?*

Gen 22:18 *And in thy seed shall all the nations of the earth be blessed; because thou hast obeyed my voice.*

Gen 17:7 *And I will establish my covenant between me and thee and thy seed after thee in their generations for an everlasting covenant, to be a God unto thee, and to thy seed after thee.*

Acts 3:22-25 *For Moses truly said unto the fathers, A prophet shall the Lord your God raise up unto you of your brethren, like unto me; him shall ye hear in all things whatsoever he shall say unto you. 23 And it shall come to pass, that every soul, which will not hear that prophet, shall be destroyed from among the people. 24 Yea, and all the prophets from Samuel and those that follow after, as many as have spoken, have likewise foretold of these days. 25 Ye are the children of the prophets, and of the covenant which God made with our fathers, saying unto Abraham, And in thy seed shall all the kindreds of the earth be blessed.*

Gal 3:29 *And if ye be Christ's, then are ye Abraham's seed, and heirs according to the promise.*

CHAPTER III

WILL THE HEAD PLEASE GO AHEAD?

Gen 2:21-25 *And the Lord God caused a deep sleep to fall upon Adam and he slept: and he took one of his ribs, and closed up the flesh instead thereof; 22 And the rib, which the Lord God had taken from man, made he a woman, and brought her unto the man. 23 And Adam said, This is now bone of my bones, and flesh of my flesh: she shall be called Woman, because she was taken out of Man. 24 Therefore shall a man leave his father and his mother, and shall cleave unto his wife: and they shall be one flesh. 25 And they were both naked, the man and his wife, and were not ashamed.*

God made preparations for Adam before He created him. God has also made preparations for us, even before we were born. It really blessed me when I understood that God prepared for me before I was born. Sometimes it may seem to us like our earthly parents did not prepare or look forward to us being born, but we must understand that our birth on this earth was no accident to God; you are not a mistake. God knew that you would be where you are right now, and He has made provisions for you. A close study of this principle helps us to understand that nothing we do surprises God. Whether right or wrong, God already knew I was going to do it, and

He knows how it is going to turn out. God foreknew what Adam would need and He created what Adam needed and had it available for him in the garden. God even foreknew that Adam would sin, and He had also made provisions for that.

Gen 1:26-27 And God said, Let us make man in our image, after our likeness: and let them have dominion over the fish of the sea, and over the fowl of the air, and over the cattle, and over all the earth, and over every creeping thing that creepeth upon the earth. 27 So God created man in his own image, in the image of God created he him; male and female created he them.

God went ahead of Adam and made preparations for him; He is the go-ahead God. Everything that Adam needed he had when God placed him in the garden. But Adam was alone and it is not good for man to be alone. God knew that Adam could not be able to fulfill his purpose being alone, just like we cannot fulfill our purpose from God being alone that is why we must learn to work together. Anything that you feel you can do alone you can rest assured that is not what called you to do.

Gen 2:18 And the Lord God said, It is not good that the man should be alone; I will make him an help meet for him.

The first thing that the go-ahead man must understand is the purpose of a wife. If we do not understand the purpose of something then we will eventually abuse it. A go-ahead man must realize that marrying a woman does not make her a wife; it only makes her a woman that is married. The Bible teaches us:

Prov 18:22 *Whoso findeth a wife findeth a good thing, and obtaineth favour of the Lord.*

The first thing I notice from Prov 18:22 is that the woman is a wife before the man finds her. When God made Eve, He made her a wife; that was her purpose. God is the only one that can make a woman a godly wife. God gave Adam a wife, Eve, to be a helpmeet to him. But what was Eve supposed to help Adam do? She was to help Adam do what God had told Adam to do, which was to tend the garden and be fruitful and multiply. God has ordained help for us; whatever God calls us to do He always sends us help. We will never be able to fulfill the call of God on our life alone; we need help from somebody. Anything that you can accomplish alone it is not your main assignment from God. The go-ahead man must obey God and do as God has commanded him to do. If the man is not doing what God has commanded him to do, then he doesn't need a helpmeet. Let's face it men—we don't need help when we are not doing what God has told us to do, we can be disobedient all by ourselves.

God CALLED Man and Man CALLED Woman

Gen 2:21-23 *And the Lord God caused a deep sleep to fall upon Adam and he slept: and he took one of his ribs, and closed up the flesh instead thereof; 22 And the rib, which the Lord God had taken from man, made he a woman,* *and brought her unto the man.23 And Adam said, This is now bone of my bones, and flesh of my flesh: she shall be called Woman, because she was taken out of Man.*

When God brought Eve to Adam, Adam immediately realized that Eve came from him and that she was a part of him. He didn't need God to tell him that; he just knew. But how did Adam know that Eve had come from him? After all, Adam was asleep when God made Eve. Adam knew that Eve came from him because Eve looked just like him, except she had a wound. God gave Adam authority over Eve, not because Adam was better or smarter than Eve, but simply because Adam was there in the garden first and God had given him the instructions. Because of the authority that Adam was given over Eve, he had the right to name her, so he called her woman, meaning *"man with a womb."* The name that Adam gave the women meant that they belonged together. This is why most men are attracted to women; that's the way God created it to be. Christ refers to this in Matthew:

Matt 19:4-6 And he answered and said unto them, Have ye not read, that he which made them at the beginning made them male and female,5 And said, For this cause shall a man leave father and mother, and shall cleave to his wife: and they twain shall be one flesh?6 Wherefore they are no more twain, but one flesh. What therefore God hath joined together, let not man put asunder.

The Word Works: So Work the Word

God took what was already in man—his rib— and made what man needed—Eve, his wife. So man already had what he needed in him, but he needed God to get it out. I realize as I study the Bible that God has placed in us abilities; we just need to allow God to draw them out. The richest place that you will ever find on earth is the graveyard because so many gifted people die without ever having manifested their gift. When God created this earth, He placed in the earth everything that man would ever need. God already foreknew our needs and desires and had already made them available for us; but we need God to help us understand how to access them.

God has gone ahead of us and made a way for us through His church. The Holy Spirit gives us a good example of how God set up His creation to work in Isa 55:10:

Isa 55:10 *For as the rain cometh down, and the snow from heaven, and returneth not thither, but watereth the earth, and maketh it bring forth and bud, that it may give seed to the sower, and bread to the eater.*

Notice that God's purpose for the rain is to *"give seed to the sower and bread to the eater."* God does not directly give us the seed or the bread. The Holy Sprirt teaches us through this passage that the earth gives seed and bread, but God sends the rain that makes the earth bring forth and bud. Notice also that the earth does not have a choice in this. The text says *"and maketh it bring forth and bud."* What I realize from this is that everything I need is already in the earth, but it only responds to God's Words. When

28

I got this revelation, I understood how important it was that I say what God has already said. Isa 55:10 teaches us how the Word of God works. His Word works just like the rain:

Isa 55:11 So shall my word be that goeth forth out of my mouth: it shall not return unto me void, but it shall accomplish that which I please, and it shall prosper in the thing whereto I sent it.

This is the same thing that God did with Adam when He created Eve. He didn't create anything new; He pulled out of man what was already in him. Notice what the Scriptures say:

Eph 1:4 According as he hath chosen us in him before the foundation of the world, that we should be holy and without blame before him in love:

Heb 4:3 For we which have believed do enter into rest, as he said, As I have sworn in my wrath, if they shall enter into my rest: although the works were finished from the foundation of the world.

1 Peter 1:18-20 Forasmuch as ye know that ye were not redeemed with corruptible things, as silver and gold, from your vain conversation received by tradition from your fathers; 19 But with the precious blood of Christ, as of a lamb without blemish and without spot: 20 Who verily was foreordained before the foundation of the world, but was manifest in these last times for you.

Does God Really Need Me?

The same way that God called woman out of man, He calls us today. I thank God every day that He called me out of a life of sin. One thing that has always fascinated me is that when I think about my life before I got saved, I realize that even when I was living in sin, God was still showing me love, and has always made a way for me. I realized that God has been with me and loved me all of my life, and I didn't even realize it. I just thought I was cool. Throughout the Bible, God has always gone ahead of man and made a way; He is our way maker. Even though God makes a way for us, we must act on faith and walk in the way that He has made. The way that God makes for us may not always be a clear path. This is why it is going to require us to walk by faith and not by sight, because if we could use our sight to see the way, then we would not need faith. God had already made a way to deliver the children of Israel, but it required Moses to walk by faith.

Ex 3:8-10 And I am come down to deliver them out of the hand of the Egyptians, and to bring them up out of that land unto a good land and a large land, unto a land flowing with milk and honey; unto the place of the Canaanites, and the Hittites, and the Amorites, and the Perizzites, and the Hivites, and the Jebusites. 9 Now therefore, behold, the cry of the children of Israel is come unto me: and I have also seen the oppression wherewith the Egyptians oppress them.10 Come now therefore, and I will send thee unto Pharaoh, that thou mayest bring forth my people the children of Israel out of Egypt.

God said He had come down and done the job, but He was sending Moses to walk in what He had done. In fact, anytime God gets ready to do anything on earth, He uses a man. The reason that God must use man is because God has given man dominion in the earth. Without God, man cannot, and without man, God will not.

Man Has Dominion

Gen 1:26 And God said; Let us make man in our image, after our likeness: and let them have dominion over the fish of the sea, and over the fowl of the air, and over the cattle, and over all the earth, and over every creeping thing that creepeth upon the earth.

Notice the two words "man" and "dominion." In order to have dominion on the earth, you must be a man or woman, meaning you must have a body. In order to have a body, you must be born of a woman. This is why Jesus had to be born of a woman. Jesus died and rose from the dead and ascended to heaven, but He kept his body!

Acts 1:11 Which also said, Ye men of Galilee, why stand ye gazing up into heaven? this same Jesus, which is taken up from you into heaven, shall so come in like manner as ye have seen him go into heaven.

The key thing to keep in mind here is that Jesus kept His body when He went to heaven, which means He still qualifies as a man and therefore has dominion on earth. Satan, on the other hand, does not have a body because he was never born of a woman. Therefore, he does not have any dominion or authority except the authority and power that man gives him. Jesus has a body because He has a birthday and Satan doesn't.

Eph 5:23 *For the husband is the head of the wife, even as Christ is the head of the church: and he is the saviour of the body.*

Adam had authority over Eve in the garden but he failed to be her savior. He was not a go-ahead man. He allowed Eve to take the head in dealing with Satan and sin came in.

Gen 3:1-6 *Now the serpent was more subtle than any beast of the field which the Lord God had made. And he said unto the woman, Yea, hath God said, Ye shall not eat of every tree of the garden?2 And the woman said unto the serpent, We may eat of the fruit of the trees of the garden:3 But of the fruit of the tree which is in the midst of the garden, God hath said, Ye shall not eat of it, neither shall ye touch it, lest ye die.4 And the serpent said unto the woman, Ye shall not surely die:5 For God doth know that in the day ye eat thereof, then your eyes shall be opened, and ye shall be as gods, knowing good and evil.6 And when the woman saw that the tree was good for food, and that it was pleasant to the eyes, and a tree to be desired to make one wise, she took of the fruit thereof, and did eat, and gave also unto her husband with her; and he did eat.*

Please notice Adam was right there with her and did not intervene. The Bible tells us that Christ is the savior of the body, "the church," and He hasn't failed and will never fail. Not only is Christ the savior of the church body but He is our personal savior. Christ saves us from sin not only because sin is bad, but because sin kills.

Rom 6:23 *For the wages of sin is death; but the gift of God is eternal life through Jesus Christ our Lord.*

Jesus wants us to live and have abundant life so He has made it so sin is powerless over us if we believe and trust in Him.

Rom 6:14 *For sin shall not have dominion over you: for ye are not under the law, but under grace.*

To the Christian, sin does not have authority over them. In other words, sin does not rule them; sin does not dictate to them, it doesn't even have any influences in their decisions. The reason God says we are not under the law is because with the law comes sin:

Rom 5:13 *For until the law sin was in the world: but sin is not imputed when there is no law.*

I know, it sounds too good to be true, but that's why it is called the Gospel, meaning *"good news or news nearly too good to be true."*

Scriptures Chapter III

Gen 2:21-25 *And the Lord God caused a deep sleep to fall upon Adam and he slept: and he took one of his ribs, and closed up the flesh instead thereof;22 And the rib, which the Lord God had taken from man, made he a woman, and brought her unto the man.23 And Adam said, This is now bone of my bones, and flesh of my flesh: she shall be called Woman, because she was taken out of Man.24 Therefore shall a man leave his father and his mother, and shall cleave unto his wife: and they shall be one flesh.25 And they were both naked, the man and his wife, and were not ashamed.*

Gen 1:26-27 *And God said, Let us make man in our image, after our likeness: and let them have dominion over the fish of the sea, and over the fowl of the air, and over the cattle, and over all the earth, and over every creeping thing that creepeth upon the earth.27 So God created man in his own image, in the image of God created he him; male and female created he them.*

Gen 2:18 *And the Lord God said, It is not good that the man should be alone; I will make him an help meet for him.*

Prov 18:22 *Whoso findeth a wife findeth a good thing, and obtaineth favour of the Lord.*

Gen.2:23 *And Adam said, This is now bone of my bones, and flesh of my flesh: she shall be called Woman, because she was taken out of Man.*

Matt 19:4-6 *And he answered and said unto them, Have ye not read, that he which made them at the beginning made them male and female,5 And said, For this cause shall a man leave father and mother, and shall cleave to his wife: and they twain shall be one flesh? 6 Wherefore they are no more twain, but one flesh. What therefore God hath joined together, let not man put asunder.*

Isa 55:10-11 *For as the rain cometh down, and the snow from heaven, and returneth not thither, but watereth the earth, and maketh it bring forth and bud, that it may give seed to the sower, and bread to the eater:11 So shall my word be that goeth forth out of my mouth: it shall not return unto me void, but it shall accomplish that which I please, and it shall prosper in the thing whereto I sent it.*

Eph 1:4 *According as he hath chosen us in him before the foundation of the world, that we should be holy and without blame before him in love.*

Heb 4:3 *For we which have believed do enter into rest, as he said, As I have sworn in my wrath, if they shall enter into my rest: although the works were finished from the foundation of the world.*

1 Peter 1:18-20 *Forasmuch as ye know that ye were not redeemed with corruptible things, as silver and gold, from your vain conversation received by tradition from your fathers;19 But with the precious blood of Christ, as of a lamb without blemish and without spot:20 Who verily was foreordained before the foundation of the world, but was manifest in these last times for you.*

Ex 3:8-10 *And I am come down to deliver them out of the hand of the Egyptians, and to bring them up out of that land unto a good land and a large land, unto a land flowing with milk and honey; unto the place of the Canaanites, and the Hittites, and the Amorites, and the Perizzites, and the Hivites, and the Jebusites.9 Now therefore, behold, the cry of the children of Israel is come unto me: and I have also seen the oppression wherewith the Egyptians oppress them.10 Come now therefore, and I will send thee unto Pharaoh, that thou mayest bring forth my people the children of Israel out of Egypt.*

Acts 1:11 *Which also said, Ye men of Galilee, why stand ye gazing up into heaven? this same Jesus, which is taken up from you into heaven, shall so come in like manner as ye have seen him go into heaven.*

Eph 5:23 *For the husband is the head of the wife, even as Christ is the head of the church: and he is the saviour of the body.*

Gen 3:1-6 *Now the serpent was more subtle than any beast of the field which the Lord God had made. And he said unto the woman, Yea, hath God said, Ye shall not eat of every tree of the garden.2 And the woman said unto the serpent, We may eat of the fruit of the trees of the garden:3 But of the fruit of the tree which is in the midst of the garden, God hath said, Ye shall not eat of it, neither shall ye touch it, lest ye die.4 And the serpent said unto the woman, Ye shall not surely die:5 For God doth know that in the day ye eat thereof, then your eyes shall be opened, and ye shall be as gods, knowing good and evil.6 And when the woman saw that the tree was good for food, and that it was pleasant to the eyes, and a tree to be desired to make one wise, she took of the fruit thereof, and did eat, and gave also unto her husband with her; and he did eat.*

Rom 6:23 *For the wages of sin is death; but the gift of God is eternal life through Jesus Christ our Lord.*

Rom 6:14 *For sin shall not have dominion over you: for ye are not under the law, but under grace.*

Rom 5:13 *(For until the law sin was in the world: but sin is not imputed when there is no law.*

CHAPTER IV

WIVES SUBMIT TO YOUR OWN HUSBAND

Col 3:18 Wives, submit yourselves unto your own husbands, as it is fit in the Lord.

Submission has become a bad word in our churches, but submission is critical to long-term success and happiness in marriage, just as it is critical for the church to submit to Christ. Submission is almost always challenged. Let's face it; nobody wants to be told what to do by someone else.

In my marriage, I had to come to the understanding that a lack of submission is a lack of obedience to God's Word. We understand that when we submit to one another, we are not submitting to the person, but we are submitting in abeyance to God's Word.

Rom 13:1-2 Let every soul be subject unto the higher powers. For there is no power but of God: the powers that be are ordained of God.2 Whosoever therefore resisteth the power, resisteth the ordinance of God: and they that resist shall receive to themselves damnation.

As Christian believers, we should always seek to obey God, and being submissive to our spouse is a great way to do that. Submission not only shows love for your spouse, more important, it shows love for Christ and abeyance to His Word.

John 14:23 *Jesus answered and said unto him, If a man love me, he will keep my words: and my Father will love him, and we will come unto him, and make our abode with him.*

Let's Take a Walk Together

I have found that I do a better job of something when I know why I am doing it. So I must ask why God wants me to submit. Is it because He knows I don't like it, and He wants me to crucify my flesh? No. Christ wants us to submit because, in marriage, the husband and wife are one, and therefore they can only go one way if they are going to walk together.

Am 3:3 *Can two walk together, except they be agreed?*

Likewise, how can we as a church walk With God unless we come into agreement with Him through submission? I believe that submission is not an issue unless there is disagreement. As long as we are in agreement, we can walk side by side. When a disagreement comes, submission is required in order to walk together.

Eph: 5:21 *Submitting yourselves one to another in the fear of God.*

37

Eph 5:24 *Therefore as the church is subject unto Christ, so let the wives be to their own husbands in everything.*

For the same reason we submit in the marriage, we also submit in the church. As the body of Christ, we must work together and follow the head, which is Christ. We may disagree at times, but we must learn to work together and become as one and submit to the head so we do not appear, in the eyes of the world, to be divided from our head. Likewise, in our homes, the husband and the wife may disagree at times, but in the eyes of their children, they cannot appear to be divided or the children will take advantage of the situation.

1 Cor 6:1 *Dare any of you, having a matter against another, go to law before the unjust, and not before the saints?*

The worldly view of submission is that it is belittling; this is simply not true. Submission is important in anything that you do if you intend on successfully completing what you are doing. If you are working with someone and there is a disagreement, then submission is required. If you are working alone and there are two or more ways you can accomplish something, then submission is required; one idea will submit to the other. Submission is so critical to our success that we must learn to accept it as a way of life. Even God submits.

Does God Really Submit?

Ps 89:34 *My covenant will I not break, nor alter the thing that is gone out of my lips.*

God must submit and be obedient to His Word. When I understood that, I realized that this can work for me or against me. This is what makes God righteous, because we know what He is going to do. Yes, God is predictable; He will do what He said in His Word He would do.

Num 23:19 *God is not a man, that he should lie; neither the son of man, that he should repent: hath he said, and shall he not do it? or hath he spoken, and shall he not make it good?*

Isa 54:8-10 *In a little wrath I hid my face from thee for a moment; but with everlasting kindness will I have mercy on thee, saith the Lord thy Redeemer.9 For this is as the waters of Noah unto me: for as I have sworn that the waters of Noah should no more go over the earth; so have I sworn that I would not be wroth with thee, nor rebuke thee.10 For the mountains shall depart, and the hills be removed; but my kindness shall not depart from thee, neither shall the covenant of my peace be removed, saith the Lord that hath mercy on thee.*

Isa 54:8-10 is one of my favorite Scriptures, because God promise in this Scripture not to be angry with me every again. In Isa 55:8 the Holy Spirit says, *"In a little wrath I hid my face from thee for a moment,"* referring to the old covenant. *"But with everlasting kindness will I have mercy on thee, saith the Lord thy Redeemer."* This part of the verse is talking about the Lord our Redeemer Jesus Christ. God, in Isa 54:9, makes us a promise and He uses the waters of Noah as an example. Just like God gave Noah the rainbow as a sign that He would not cover the earth with water any more, God gave us a sign in Isa 54:10 that He would not be angry with us any more. *"For the mountains shall depart, and the hills be removed; but my kindness shall not depart from thee, neither shall the covenant of my peace be removed, saith the Lord that hath mercy on thee."*

The Holy Spirit tells us that even though the hills and the mountains may be removed, God's covenant of peace would not. If you ever wonder whether or not God is angry with you, look for a hill or a mountain. We can usually find a hill or a mountain, but even if we can't base on this scripture God is still not angry with you.

Did Jesus Submit?

Christ, the Son of God, submits to the Father:

Matt 26:39 And he went a little further, and fell on his face, and prayed, saying, O my Father, if it be possible, let this cup pass from me: nevertheless not as I will, but as thou wilt.

Mark 14:36 And he said, Abba, Father, all things are possible unto thee; take away this cup from me: nevertheless not what I will, but what thou wilt.

Luke 22:42 Saying, Father, if thou be willing, remove this cup from me: nevertheless not my will, but thine, be done.

Jesus said, *"Not my will, but thine, be done."* Jesus' focus was on doing the Father's will; He wanted to please the Father. Based on the Bible, I believe it is safe to say that Jesus was not thrilled about going to the cross, but He humbled Himself to the cross. Jesus knew that the Father loved Him and that the Father wanted to show His love for man through Him. He had man's best interest in mind. I don't know about you, but some of the things that God's Word commands, I didn't find too appealing at first. But because I know that God loves me and that He has my best interest in mind, I submit freely to His Word.

As Christians, we should live a lifestyle that is subject to God's Word, and the only way we can do that is to get a revelation of God's love. The Bible teaches us that wives are to be subject to their husbands in everything "as the church is subject to Christ in everything." The question I ask as a husband is, "How does Christ get the church to be subject to Him?" The answer is, with love and kindness.

Jer 31:3 The Lord hath appeared of old unto me, saying, Yea, I have loved thee with an everlasting love: therefore with lovingkindness have I drawn thee.

He Loves Me? Or He Loves Me Not?

Unfortunately, most Christians do not understand what unconditional love is. When the husband doesn't show unconditional love to the wife, then the wife has a problem submitting to the husband. The church must submit to Christ freely and willingly, out of love; that is the way the wife submits to her husband. The Bible gives the wife a command: *"Wives, submit to your husbands."* Note that this command is given to the wives, not to the husbands; likewise, the command is given to the church. Wives are commanded to submit to their husbands. The husband cannot force his wife to submit; submission is always freely given. Nowhere in the Bible are husbands given any authority to force their wives to submit. The command to love in this text is given to the husband only because submission comes more easily for the husband, just as love comes more easily for the wife. By commanding the wife to submit and the husband to love, God is calling them both to sacrifice.

Christ will not force the church to submit to Him. It must be freely given, for forced submission is not true submission. Even though submission is commanded for the wife, her compliance is *voluntary*. As long as the husband is fulfilling his responsibility and loving his wife, the same way that Christ loved the church, the wife has the responsibility to submit to him "in everything." If she fails to do so, she is accountable not so much to her husband but to God. The same is true with the church's submission to Christ; it must be *voluntary*. We know that Christ has fulfilled his responsibility to the church so the church has the responsibility to submit to him "in everything."

Why Won't My Wife Submit To Me?

Husbands, the most well-kept secret are how to get your wife to submit to you. The answer is love. Because security is the most important thing to a woman, she must know you love her and that you have her best interest foremost on your mind as you make daily decisions. If she knows this, she will be happy to submit to you. Let's look at how we as a church submit to Christ. First we must be obedient and recognize Christ as our head and we, the church, as his body. As the body of Christ (the church), we recognize that Christ loves us and in loving us, He wants the best for us. Therefore, we submit to Him.

Eph 5:29 *For no man ever yet hated his own flesh; but nourisheth and cherisheth it, even as the Lord the church.*

When we recognize that Christ loves us and is obviously capable of meeting our needs, we should have no problem submitting to Him.

Phil 4:19 *But my God shall supply all your need according to his riches in glory by Christ Jesus.*

Eph 3:20 *Now unto him that is able to do exceeding abundantly above all that we ask or think, according to the power that worketh in us.*

As a wife, you might say, "That sounds great when you talk about Jesus, but what about my husband?" As a wife, you must have the attitude that your husband has been called to be your husband. No one can do anything better than someone doing what they have been called by God to do. The man was given the headship by God and whether the wife submits or not, the husband is still the head. Suppose we did not recognize Christ as the head of the church. Would that mean He is not the head? Of course not.

Rom 8:30 *Moreover whom he did predestinate, them he also called: and whom he called, them he also justified: and whom he justified, them he also glorified.*

Notice the Scripture says whom He *called*. That does not mean to *summons*; rather, it means to *identify*. God calls us to be what He created us to be. Even though we may not be where God called us to be presently, God recognizes us as being in the position He called us to. God has identified the husband as the head and has given him the Grace to operate in the calling of headship. There are times that the man will be able to accomplish things that the women cannot just because of the grace that God has placed on his life. Whatever God calls someone to do; He gives them the Grace to be able to do it.

In a Christian marriage, a lack of submission to each other means a lack of trust in God and a lack of trust in His Word. What we are really saying when we don't submit one to another is, "God, I don't trust you, and I have to look out for myself." If you have ever wondered about your maturity as a Christian, ask yourself, "Do I have a problem with submission?" If you answer "yes," God will help you when you ask Him. If you answer "no," that's great. We must understand that God is our creator; He created the union of marriage just like He created the institution of the church, so He knows what it takes to make a marriage work. Likewise, He knows what it takes to make His church work. We must do marriage God's way, starting with picking a Godly mate.

2 Cor 6:14 Be ye not unequally yoked together with unbelievers: for what fellowship hath righteousness with unrighteousness? and what communion hath light with darkness?

The Perfect Church Building and the Perfect Mate

Let me help you by saying there is no perfect mate! Likewise, there is no perfect church. If you find a church that you think is perfect don't join it because something is not right with it. You choose a Godly mate and make a commitment to each other to make it work with the help of God. The same is true with your church building. This is why it is so important to do it God's way because when we start off the right way, with the help of God, we will end up in the right place. Remember, God blessed the union of marriage, just like He blessed His church. We must allow the Lord to lead us when choosing our mate as well as our place of worship because God only blesses what He has called. God will not bless sin.

If you are like most Christians, you got married at a young age while you were unsaved. Since then you have received Christ into your life and now you find yourself struggling to make your marriage work. If your mate is seeking the same things you are, that is a good thing; just lock in and work the Word. But if you are trying to make the marriage work and your spouse isn't, then you are in the perfect position to trust God. The main thing we must ask ourselves about submission is, "Do I believe what the Bible says about submission or not?" because we are really submitting to God's Word.

Satan seeks to overthrow God's kingdom by getting us to doubt God's Word. Satan knows if he gets two people unequally yoked together, it will disrupt the home, which will disrupt the church. In turn this will disrupt the city, then the country, and finally the kingdom. Thank God his plan is not going to work.

SCRIPTURES CHAPTER IV

Col 3:18 *Wives, submit yourselves unto your own husbands, as it is fit in the Lord.*

Rom 13:1-2 *Let every soul be subject unto the higher powers. For there is no power but of God: the powers that be are ordained of God; 2 Whosoever therefore resisteth the power, resisteth the ordinance of God: and they that resist shall receive to themselves damnation.*

John 14:23 *Jesus answered and said unto him, If a man love me, he will keep my words: and my Father will love him, and we will come unto him, and make our abode with him.*

Am 3:3 *Can two walk together, except they be agreed?*

Eph 5:21 *Submitting yourselves one to another in the fear of God.*

Eph 5:24 *Therefore as the church is subject unto Christ, so let the wives be to their own husbands in every thing.*

1 Cor 6:1 *Dare any of you, having a matter against another, go to law before the unjust, and not before the saints?*

Ps 89:34 *My covenant will I not break, nor alter the thing that is gone out of my lips.*

Num 23:19 *God is not a man, that he should lie; neither the son of man, that he should repent: hath he said, and shall he not do it? or hath he spoken, and shall he not make it good?*

Isa 54:8-10 *In a little wrath I hid my face from thee for a moment; but with everlasting kindness will I have mercy on thee, saith the Lord thy Redeemer.9 For this is as the waters of Noah unto me: for as I have sworn that the waters of Noah should no more go over the earth; so have I sworn that I would not be wroth with thee, nor rebuke thee.10 For the mountains shall depart, and the hills be removed; but my kindness shall not depart from thee, neither shall the covenant of my peace be removed, saith the Lord that hath mercy on thee.*

Matt 26:39 *And he went a little further, and fell on his face, and prayed, saying, O my Father, if it be possible, let this cup pass from me: nevertheless not as I will, but as thou wilt.*

Mark 14:36 *And he said, Abba, Father, all things are possible unto thee; take away this cup from me: nevertheless not what I will, but what thou wilt.*

Luke 22:42 *Saying, Father, if thou be willing, remove this cup from me: nevertheless not my will, but thine, be done.*

Jer 31:3 *The Lord hath appeared of old unto me, saying, Yea, I have loved thee with an everlasting love: therefore with lovingkindness have I drawn thee.*

Eph 5:29 *For no man ever yet hated his own flesh; but nourisheth and cherisheth it, even as the Lord the church.*

Phil 4:19 *But my God shall supply all your need according to his riches in glory by Christ Jesus.*

Eph 3:20 *Now unto him that is able to do exceeding abundantly above all that we ask or think, according to the power that worketh in us.*

Rom 8:30 *Moreover whom he did predestinate, them he also called: and whom he called, them he also justified: and whom he justified, them he also glorified.*

2 Cor 6:14 *Be ye not unequally yoked together with unbelievers: for what fellowship hath righteousness with unrighteousness? and what communion hath light with darkness?*

CHAPTER V

HUSBANDS LOVE YOUR WIVES

Have you ever wondered why God commanded the wife to submit to her husband and commanded the husband to love his wife? Simply put, husbands usually do not have a problem submitting to their wives; most husbands are content going alone with what their wives say. But the husband needs help in learning how to show love and romance to the wife. On the other hand, love and romance usually come naturally to the wife, but she may have difficulty with submission.

One of the main reasons that God gave man free will was so that man could love Him. God knows that every time He creates a human being, He is taking a chance that that person will not love Him. But He also knows that if He is to experience true love from man, He must let man go and allow man to come to Him willingly. God showed His love for man by giving His son for our sins. Jesus showed his love by submitting to the will of the Father and going to the cross. As the church, the body of Christ, the only appropriate response to the love of God is submission.

I believe that if there were one word to describe God, it would be love. The Bible says God *is* love:

1 John 4:8 He that loveth not knoweth not God; for God is love.

God does not simply have love or show love, He is love, and therefore due submission from all. Just as God shows love to His church, so must husbands and wives show love to each other.

Till Death Do Us Part

I do not believe that anyone goes into a marriage with the intention of divorce, but without God, man is incapable of true love because God is love. The greatest thing that any marriage or any person can possess is the love of God or, you could say, the God kind of love.

I Cor. 13:13 And now abide faith, hope, love, these three; but the greatest of these is love.

Before we look at what the God kind of love is, let's look at what the God kind of love is not. The God kind of love is not a feeling or an emotion. Jesus teaches us:

Matt 5:44 But I say unto you, Love your enemies, bless them that curse you, do good to them that hate you, and pray for them which despitefully use you, and persecute you.

I don't know about you, but I don't think I am ever going to feel like loving my enemies. Jesus expects us to love our enemies, and the only way that is going to happen is if we make a decision to love them. If I allow my feelings to guide me, I will never be able to love my enemies. Allowing our feelings to guide us is one of the biggest mistakes Christians can make. Feelings are great, but they should not be our guide. That is not why God gave them to us.

Rom 8:14 *For as many as are led by the Spirit of God, they are the sons of God.*

Guiding us is the job of the Holy Spirit, not feelings. Unfortunately, most people are led by their five senses: taste, sight, touch, hearing, speech. Our senses have a purpose, but they are not a guide to life. Their purpose is mostly for the protection of our body. God created man to dwell in a physical world, so he needed a physical body. God gave man's physical body senses—or you could say sensors—to help keep him safe by making him aware of his surroundings. If you eat something that could possibly be harmful to your body, your sense of taste instantly lets you know. The same is true with sight; if you see danger, you move away from it. All five of our senses are continuously monitoring our surrounding. The sound of a car horn makes us take notice.

We cannot afford to make decisions in life based on how we feel. If we allow our feelings to influence us, then they will shape the way we think. How we think is important because it is going to be the determining factor in our decisions. The decisions we make determine our actions, and our actions determine what we get out of life. The biggest danger in allowing your feelings to lead you is that feelings change, and sometimes without notice. If you make a life alerting decision today based on feelings and tomorrow you feel differently, then you have a big problem. When we begin to live a life of the love of God, we must learn how to respond to our feelings and make a decision to show the love of God. To really understand what the God kind of love is, we must go to the love chapter in the Bible: I Cor 13.

What's Love Got To Do With It?

1 Cor 13:1-8 Though I speak with the tongues of men and of angels, and have not charity, I am become as sounding brass, or a tinkling cymbal.2 And though I have the gift of prophecy, and understand all mysteries, and all knowledge; and though I have all faith, so that I could remove mountains, and have not charity, I am nothing.3 And though I bestow all my goods to feed the poor, and though I give my body to be burned, and have not charity, it profiteth me nothing.4 Charity suffereth long, and is kind; charity envieth not; charity vaunteth not itself, is not puffed up,5 Doth not behave itself unseemly, seeketh not her own, is not easily provoked, thinketh no evil;6 Rejoiceth not in iniquity, but rejoiceth in the truth;7 Beareth all things, believeth all things, hopeth all things, endureth all things.

8 Charity never faileth: but whether there be prophecies, they shall fail; whether there be tongues, they shall cease; whether there be knowledge, it shall vanish away.

The Holy Sprit teaches us in I Cor 13:1 that everything we do should be done out of love. The Spirit even goes so far as to say that if we don't do it out of love, then what we do is worthless. After reading this, one might become confused, and say, "If I do something for someone it is not worthless to the person I do it for." You may be right, but in God's eyes, it is worthless. He will not be able to reward you for it, and God wants the giver to be rewarded, as well as the receiver. Everything that God asks us to do in the Bible will lead us to prosper.

3 John 2 Beloved, I wish above all things that thou mayest prosper and be in health, even as thy soul prospereth.

The Spirit of God goes on to say that our God-given abilities, our gifts, must be used in love or else they are worthless. Even though our gifts and abilities come from God, we can make them worthless by not using them in love. This is why most people, even Christians, are not seeing the promises of God manifest in there lives, because everything in the Bible operates by love, even our faith.

Gal.5:6 For in Jesus Christ neither circumcision availeth anything, nor uncircumcision; but faith which worketh by love.

Could this be the reason so many Christians are not seeing the promises of God come into their life? Faith works by love and when there is no love, faith doesn't work. We need working faith to please God, and pleasing the Father should be our main goal. Let face it, when you love someone, you want to please them. God tells us how to please Him—just believe Him. I think that you would find it very difficult to please anyone that you didn't believe. How do you think your spouse would feel if you told them, "Honey I love you, but I don't believe a word you say."

I Cor. 13:3 And though I bestow all my goods to feed the poor, and though I give my body to be burned, and have not charity, it profiteth me nothing.

Everything we do must be done out of a heart of love in order to be a benefit to the giver. God's desire is for His people to benefit in everything that they do. For the natural man, doing everything in love is impossible. But Christians are not natural; they are supernatural.

2 Cor 9:7 Every man according as he purposeth in his heart, so let him give; not grudgingly, or of necessity: for God loveth a cheerful giver.

In I Cor 13:4, the Holy Spirit begins to talk about the characteristics of love. Knowing the characteristics of love is important to us so we will be able to recognize love when we see it. In I Cor 13:1-3, the Spirit talks about love as it refers to giving. Most of us can easily recognize love when it is giving, because we know that love always gives. John 3:16 teaches us that God so loved the world that He gave His only son.

Giving is great, but giving is not the only thing that love does. The text says, *"Charity suffereth long."* Some people might say it like this, "Love is blind." Simply put, love will put up with things that hurt. I'm sure at one time or another you have been hurt by someone you loved, but you got over it and stayed in the relationship because you loved them. It is a lot easier to stay on course when love is present. The Spirit goes on to say that love is kind, even while suffering. This makes a world of difference. Most of the time when we suffer we have no choice in the matter, but to be kind while we suffer—WOW!

Love is the one thing that everyone responds to and seeks. What we are really seeking, even if we don't realize it, is God, because God is love. God has placed the desire for love in everything that He has created. Human beings want love so badly that we accept cheap imitations. This is why we get involved in all kinds of sinful things; we are looking for love in all the wrongs places. Even our pets and plants respond to love. There is no imitation for the God kind of love; it will always make itself known. Notice in Gen 26:8-9, Isaac tries to pass off Rebekah as his sister. But because he loved her, Abimelech knew who she was by just a glance out of the window.

Gen 26:8-9 And it came to pass, when he had been there a long time, that Abimelech king of the Philistines looked out at a window, and saw, and, behold, Isaac was sporting with Rebekah his wife. 9 And Abimelech called Isaac, and said, Behold, of a surety she is thy wife: and how saidst thou, She is my sister? And Isaac said unto him, Because I said, Lest I die for her.

Remember husbands, agape love always puts your wife's needs before yours. If you say, "My wife doesn't submit to me the way she should," then you must ask yourself the question, "Do I love my wife the way I should?" To the degree that you show agape love to your wife, that is the degree she will submit to you. Let's take a moment and review what love is.

1 Cor 13:4-8 Love suffers long and is kind; love does not envy; love does not parade itself, is not puffed up; 5 does not behave rudely, does not seek its own, is not provoked, thinks no evil; 6 does not rejoice in iniquity, but rejoices in the truth; 7 bears all things, believes all things, hopes all things, endures all things. 8 Charity never faileth: but whether there be prophecies, they shall fail; whether there be tongues, they shall cease; whether there be knowledge, it shall vanish away.

Notice what it does *not* say; it does not put any stipulation on the other person. It doesn't matter what the other person does; you must continue to love them. I know that's a hard pill to swallow, but that's agape love, better known as the love of God, or the love that comes from God, or the God kind of love. As a go-ahead man, you have to make up your mind and say, "I am going to love my wife, and it doesn't matter how she acts or how she treats me." Then you will begin to experience a godly marriage as you practice the God kind of love. So go ahead and be a go-ahead man, loving your wife the way Christ loved the church.

SCRIPTURES CHAPTER V

1 John 4:8 *He that loveth not knoweth not God; for God is love.*

1 Cor 13:13 *And now abideth faith, hope, charity, these three; but the greatest of these is charity.*

Matt 5:44 *But I say unto you, Love your enemies, bless them that curse you, do good to them that hate you, and pray for them which despitefully use you, and persecute you.*

Rom 8:14 *For as many as are led by the Spirit of God, they are the sons of God.*

1 Cor 13:1-8 *Though I speak with the tongues of men and of angels, and have not charity, I am become as sounding brass, or a tinkling cymbal.2 And though I have the gift of prophecy, and understand all mysteries, and all knowledge; and though I have all faith, so that I could remove mountains, and have not charity, I am nothing.3 And though I bestow all my goods to feed the poor, and though I give my body to be burned, and have not charity, it profiteth me nothing.4 Charity suffereth long, and is kind; charity envieth not; charity vaunteth not itself, is not puffed up, 5 Doth not behave itself unseemly, seeketh not her own, is not easily provoked, thinketh no evil;6 Rejoiceth not in iniquity, but rejoiceth in the truth;7 Beareth all things, believeth all things, hopeth all things, endureth all things.8 Charity never faileth: but whether there be prophecies, they shall fail; whether there be tongues, they shall cease; whether there be knowledge, it shall vanish away.*

3 John 2 *Beloved, I wish above all things that thou mayest prosper and be in health, even as thy soul prospereth.*

Gal 5:6 *For in Jesus Christ neither circumcision availeth anything, nor uncircumcision; but faith which worketh by love.*

I Cor. 13:3 *And though I bestow all my goods to feed the poor, and though I give my body to be burned, and have not charity, it profiteth me nothing.*

2 Cor 9:7 *Every man according as he purposeth in his heart, so let him give; not grudgingly, or of necessity: for God loveth a cheerful giver.*

Gen 26:8-9 *And it came to pass, when he had been there a long time, that Abimelech king of the Philistines looked out at a window, and saw, and, behold, Isaac was sporting with Rebekah his wife.9 And Abimelech called Isaac, and said, Behold, of a surety she is thy wife: and how saidst thou, She is my sister? And Isaac said unto him, Because I said, Lest I die for her.*

1 Cor 13:4-8 *Love suffers long and is kind; love does not envy; love does not parade itself, is not puffed up; 5 does not behave rudely, does not seek its own, is not provoked, thinks no evil; 6 does not rejoice in iniquity, but rejoices in the truth; 7 bears all things, believes all things, hopes all things, endures all things. 8 Charity never faileth: but whether there be prophecies, they shall fail; whether there be tongues, they shall cease; whether there be knowledge, it shall vanish away.*

CHAPTER VI

CHRIST LOVED THE CHURCH

Eph 5:25 Husbands, love your wives, even as Christ also loved the church, and gave himself for it.

This text not only commands husbands to love their wives, but it tells them how to love their wives: the same way Christ loved the church. Christ shows unconditional love for His church. This gives husbands a great goal to reach for. Christ not only showed his love by dying on the cross, but He continues to show His love for His church daily. Likewise, the husband not only shows his love for his wife on their wedding day, but he must continue to show his love for her daily. Let's take a look at how Christ loves the church. The Spirit of God puts this in a way that we can relate to and understand.

Eph 5:28 So ought men to love their wives as their own bodies. He that loveth his wife loveth himself.

The first thing I learn from this is that the man must love himself. If the man does not love himself, he will never be able to show his wife the God kind of love. The Holy Spirit's focus here is that the husband deals with the wife's flesh the same way he deals with his own flesh. The husband in a sense takes the wife's body and gives her his body, and this is how they deal with each other. In other words, they trade places. This sounds familiar, doesn't it? Christ traded places with us. He became sin so that we could become the righteousness of God; Christ took our place.

2 Cor 5:21 *For he hath made him to be sin for us, who knew no sin; that we might be made the righteousness of God in him.*

2 Cor 8:9 *For ye know the grace of our Lord Jesus Christ, that, though he was rich, yet for your sakes he became poor, that ye through his poverty might be rich.*

This also helps us understand why the church is called the body of Christ. Christ loved the church the same way He loved Himself. One might say, "Well, the Bible doesn't say anything about God loving Himself." Let's take a closer look. First of all, God tells us to love ourselves in Lev. 19:18.

Lev 19:18 *Thou shalt not avenge, nor bear any grudge against the children of thy people, but thou shalt love thy neighbour as thyself: I am the Lord.*

Just as we are to love our neighbour as ourselves God also loves himself. God loved Himself so much that He recreated Himself in us; I believe that is why God made us in His likeness and in His image.

Gen 1:26 *And God said, Let us make man in our image, after our likeness: and let them have dominion over the fish of the sea, and over the fowl of the air, and over the cattle, and over all the earth, and over every creeping thing that creepeth upon the earth.*

This is one of the reasons the love of God is so great toward man—because we are like God Himself. God Himself calls us gods (little "g" of course):

Psalm 82:6 *I have said, Ye are gods; and all of you are children of the most High.*

God's relationship with man has been misunderstood even by some of the men of God in the Old Testament:

Ps 8:4-8 *What is man, that thou art mindful of him? and the son of man, that thou visitest him?5 For thou hast made him a little lower than the angels, and hast crowned him with glory and honour.6 Thou madest him to have dominion over the works of thy hands; thou hast put all things under his feet:7 All sheep and oxen, yea, and the beasts of the field;8 The fowl of the air, and the fish of the sea, and whatsoever passeth through the paths of the seas.*

Chip Off the Old Block

When we try to understand why God does what He does, it doesn't make any sense to our natural mind, but we know we like it. Our goal in life is to be like our Father; this is our call and what we are working toward. To understand this, we must have some understanding of the concept of spirit, soul, and body. When we get saved, we get a new spirit. Our soul is where our mind resides; this is why we are in a constant state of renewing our mind. Our body is just the house that we live in, and it is also part of our flesh. Our flesh is and will be our greatest problem until we get our new bodies, so thank God we have a God over our flesh.

Jer 32:27 Behold, I am the Lord, the God of all flesh: is there anything too hard for me?

Rom 8:29 For whom he did foreknow, he also did predestinate to be conformed to the image of his Son, that he might be the firstborn among many brethren.

Satan knows this and this is why he is our enemy—we have achieved merely by being created what he tried, but failed, to get by sinning. God created us to be like Him and the entire spirit world knows this. Unfortunately, we as Christians haven't realized it yet.

Isa 14:13-14 For thou hast said in thine heart, I will ascend into heaven, I will exalt my throne above the stars of God: I will sit also upon the mount of the congregation, in the sides of the north: I will ascend above the heights of the clouds; I will be like the most High.

Satan's desire was, and is, to be like God, but that will never be because Satan was not created in God's image or likeness. Satan knows he cannot be God of the universe so he tries to be god over man, and he uses three things to accomplish this: lust of the eye, lust of the flesh, and pride of life. We as Christians, on the other hand, have a calling to be like God: now we see why Satan hates us so much.

Eph 5:1 *Be ye therefore followers of God, as dear children.*

The word "follow" means "*to imitate*" and imitating speaks of a process. Our heavenly Father does not give us anything before we are ready. I truly believe that if Adam and Eve had waited, God would have made the tree of life available to them.

1 Cor 13:11-12 *When I was a child, I spake as a child, I understood as a child, I thought as a child: but when I became a man, I put away childish things.12 For now we see through a glass, darkly; but then face to face: now I know in part; but then shall I know even as also I am known.*

This is how Satan was able to trick Eve in the garden; he made her think she could be like God without going thru the process and waiting on God.

We All Were Stillborn

Gen 3:5 *For God doth know that in the day ye eat thereof, then your eyes shall be opened, and ye shall be as gods, knowing good and evil.*

When Adam fell in the garden, sin begin to reign and man died spiritually. Everyone born after Adam was born in sin and spiritually dead. This is why Jesus told Nicodemus in John 3:7:

John 3:7 Marvel not that I said unto thee, Ye must be born again.

Being born again, according to Rom. 8:11, quickens our spirit and we once again become in the likeness and image of God.

Rom 8:11 But if the Spirit of him that raised up Jesus from the dead dwell in you, he that raised up Christ from the dead shall also quicken your mortal bodies by his Spirit that dwelleth in you.

Tit 3:3-5 For we ourselves also were sometimes foolish, disobedient, deceived, serving divers lusts and pleasures, living in malice and envy, hateful, and hating one another.4 But after that the kindness and love of God our Saviour toward man appeared,5 Not by works of righteousness which we have done, but according to his mercy he saved us, by the washing of regeneration, and renewing of the Holy Ghost;

The church is the body of Christ, so as Christ loves the church He loves Himself. Likewise, as the husband loves his wife, he loves himself. If you want to know what the husband is like, look at the wife. If you want to know what the wife is like, look at the husband. Most Christians don't recognize this, but we see it throughout the Bible. The world looks at us when they want to know what God is like. This is why it is important that we check ourselves.

Eph 5:31 *For this cause shall a man leave his father and mother, and shall be joined unto his wife, and they two shall be one flesh.*

Eph 5:26 *That he might sanctify and cleanse it with the washing of water by the word.*

In Eph 5:26, look at how Christ takes care of his body or his church. First, He sets it apart for Himself. That is what makes the church holy, because it is set apart for God's use. Likewise, the husband sets his wife apart for himself; she should be his only woman. Christ assumes the responsibility of cleansing the church. Notice how Christ cleans the church and what He uses to clean it—the Word of God. God speaks the Word over his church. Likewise, the husband speaks over the life of his wife and family. This is not how we traditionally look at marriage, but tradition is very dangerous when it come to the things of God.

Matt 15:6 *And honour not his father or his mother, he shall be free. Thus have ye made the commandment of God of none effect by your tradition.*

A Present for Himself

Christ takes such good care of His church because He is going to present it to Himself. This is the same attitude the husband must have. The husband must look at his wife as if he is going to present her to himself.

Eph 5:27 *That he might present it to himself a glorious church, not having spot, or wrinkle, or any such thing; but that it should be holy and without blemish.*

Christ is not going to present just any church to Himself; He is going to make sure it is a glorious church, one that is clean without spot or wrinkle. Look at the care Christ takes with His church, note the love He puts into it. He makes it holy and without blemish. Husbands love your body and keep it looking good. Remember, the head can accomplish nothing without the body.

Can you imagine what your life would be like if your body and your head were not in agreement with each other? Your head could be thinking one thing and your body doing something else. Suppose you were driving down the road and your arms decided to turn the steering wheel without your head's permission; you would not have a good day. Maybe one day while you are shopping your body decides, "I am going to the bathroom now." Simply put you would be considered sick. I wonder how many sick marriages are in the world, with the head thinking one thing and the body doing something else. Don't let your marriage be one of those sick marriages.

SCRIPTURES CHAPTER VI

Eph 5:25 *Husbands, love your wives, even as Christ also loved the church, and gave himself for it.*

Eph 5:28 *So ought men to love their wives as their own bodies. He that loveth his wife loveth himself.*

2 Cor 5:21 *For he hath made him to be sin for us, who knew no sin; that we might be made the righteousness of God in him.*

2 Cor 8:9 *For ye know the grace of our Lord Jesus Christ, that, though he was rich, yet for your sakes he became poor, that ye through his poverty might be rich.*

Lev 19:18 *Thou shalt not avenge, nor bear any grudge against the children of thy people, but thou shalt love thy neighbour as thyself: I am the Lord.*

Gen 1:26 *And God said, Let us make man in our image, after our likeness: and let them have dominion over the fish of the sea, and over the fowl of the air, and over the cattle, and over all the earth, and over every creeping thing that creepeth upon the earth.*

Ps 82:6 *I have said, Ye are gods; and all of you are children of the most High.*

Ps 8:4-8 *What is man, that thou art mindful of him? and the son of man, that thou visitest him? 5 For thou hast made him a little lower than the angels, and hast crowned him with glory and honour. 6 Thou madest him to have dominion over the works of thy hands; thou hast put all things under his feet: 7 All sheep and oxen, yea, and the beasts of the field; The fowl of the air, and the fish of the sea, and whatsoever passeth through the paths of the seas.*

Jer 32:27 *Behold, I am the Lord, the God of all flesh: is there any thing too hard for me?*

Rom 8:29 *For whom he did foreknow, he also did predestinate to be conformed to the image of his Son, that he might be the firstborn among many brethren.*

Isa 14:13-14 *For thou hast said in thine heart, I will ascend into heaven, I will exalt my throne above the stars of God: I will sit also upon the mount of the congregation, in the sides of the north:14 I will ascend above the heights of the clouds; I will be like the most High.*

Eph 5:1 *Be ye therefore followers of God, as dear children.*

1 Cor 13:11-12 *When I was a child, I spake as a child, I understood as a child, I thought as a child: but when I became a man, I put away childish things.12 For now we see* *through a glass, darkly; but then face to face: now I know in part; but then shall I know even as also I am known.*

Gen 3:5 *For God doth know that in the day ye eat thereof, then your eyes shall be opened, and ye shall be as gods, knowing good and evil.*

John 3:7 *Marvel not that I said unto thee, Ye must be born again.*

Rom 8:11 *But if the Spirit of him that raised up Jesus from the dead dwell in you, he that raised up Christ from the dead shall also quicken your mortal bodies by his Spirit that dwelleth in you.*

Tit 3:3-5 *For we ourselves also were sometimes foolish, disobedient, deceived, serving diverse lusts and pleasures, living in malice and envy, hateful, and hating one another.4 But after that the kindness and love of God our Saviour toward man appeared,5 Not by works of righteousness which we have done, but according to his mercy he saved us, by the washing of regeneration, and renewing of the Holy Ghost.*

Eph 5:31 *For this cause shall a man leave his father and mother, and shall be joined unto his wife, and they two shall be one flesh.*

Matt 15:6 *And honour not his father or his mother, he shall be free. Thus have ye made the commandment of God of none effect by your tradition.*

Eph 5:26 *That he might sanctify and cleanse it with the washing of water by the word.*

Eph 5:27 *That he might present it to himself a glorious church, not having spot, or wrinkle, or any such thing; but that it should be holy and without blemish.*

CHAPTER VII

CHRIST GAVE HIMSELF FOR THE CHURCH

I am sure you realize by now that the church is not the building, it is Christ's body. Or you could say that born-again believers make up the church. To become part of God's church; we simply must be born again, meaning that we must believe in Jesus Christ as our Lord and Savior. When we believe in Jesus Christ as our Lord and Savior, we are joined to Christ's church. You may not have gotten saved in a church, but the day you believed, you became part of the body of Christ, the called out ones, the church. You may not have signed a roll or repeated a creed or even shook the pastor's hand, but when you said yes to Jesus as the Lord and Savior of your life, you became part of Him by being joined to his body, the church. I accepted Christ into my life while watching a sermon on TV. I didn't feel any goose bumps or pass out or anything. I simply made up my mind, "God, I am going to try you, because nothing else is working." Once I made up my mind, God slowly began to reveal Himself to me. Now eighteen years later, I am still in the process of getting to know God, but I was joined to His body the moment I said yes to Him.

What God Has Joined Together Let Not Man Put Asunder

Matt 19:6 *Wherefore they are no more twain, but one flesh. What therefore God hath joined together, let not man put asunder.*

This Scripture is one we often hear at weddings, and rightfully so, but it also applies to the body of Christ. Christ has perfectly and purposely joined his body together into the church. As Christ's church, we must understand what our purpose is. Christ did not simply join us together so we could get together and have a good time running up and down the aisles of the church building. Although that is a lot of fun, we have a deeper purpose. We as the church represent Jesus. As a church, we should be able to work together and accomplish anything in Christ Jesus. The Bible also teaches us in Phil. 4:13 that:

Phil 4:13 *I can do all things through Christ which strengtheneth me.*

In order for us, the body, to be effective, we must stay connected to Christ, the head. As the church, we must remember that Christ is our source. Christ is where we get our directions from, and we can do nothing without Him, just like you can do nothing without your physical body. The reason it is so important that the whole body recognize Christ as the head is because then we all will get our directions from the same place, and we can operate in unity.

John 15:5 *I am the vine, ye are the branches: He that abideth in me, and I in him, the same bringeth forth much fruit: for without me ye can do nothing.*

69

It is essential for the members of our body to work together in order to accomplish our daily tasks. Likewise, it is essential for Christ's body to work together to accomplish God's will on earth. As the body of Christ, it is our job to walk in the Spirit of God, and only then will we make God's enemies His footstool.

Heb 1:13 But to which of the angels said he at any time, Sit on my right hand, until I make thine enemies thy footstool?

Likewise, the husband and the wife must learn to function as one. This is why Jesus declared that the two shall become one. The go-ahead man must also realize that there is no more yours and mine; everything is us and ours because they are one. Being one does not mean that you are going to think alike and always agree with each other. But in the end, you must manifest one goal and have one direction, just as you as an individual can have many ideas and many thoughts, but can only do them well one at a time. Being one means being whole or complete, which means if you take anything away, it will not function the way God intended. This is why Paul said:

Rom 8:38-39 For I am persuaded, that neither death, nor life, nor angels, nor principalities, nor powers, nor things present, nor things to come, nor height, nor depth, nor any other creature, shall be able to separate us from the love of God, which is in Christ Jesus our Lord.

The Power of Agreement

Two functioning as one, or two in agreement, is a powerful combination. The Bible teaches:

Am 3:3 Can two walk together, except they be agreed?

Agreement is not only powerful, but it is also necessary if two people are to walk together. Agreement is so powerful that it moves God and heaven. Look at what Jesus said in Matthew:

Matt 18:18-20 Verily I say unto you, Whatsoever ye shall bind on earth shall be bound in heaven: and whatsoever ye shall loose on earth shall be loosed in heaven.19 Again I say unto you, That if two of you shall agree on earth as touching any thing that they shall ask, it shall be done for them of my Father which is in heaven.20 For where two or three are gathered together in my name, there am I in the midst of them.

Please notice the advantages we have when we are in agreement. When we come into agreement and do things on earth, this causes things to happen in heaven. Whatever we do in agreement on earth, the same is done for us in heaven. This is a very important law, and it can work for us or against us, depending on what we agree on. For this reason, you should never agree with anything or anyone that is not speaking the will of God for your life. Another great thing that happens when we agree is that Jesus comes in the midst. As Christians, we have learned from experience that when Jesus is in the midst, everything is going to be all right. I believe that the reason Jesus comes in the midst of agreement is because when we agree, Jesus can bring peace into the situation. Jesus takes a personal interest in two or three in agreement so much so that He comes in the midst, and brings peace: perhaps this is why He is called the Prince of Peace.

I Give Myself Away

Just as Christ gave Himself for the church, the go-ahead man gives himself for his wife. Notice that Christ did not give Himself *to* the church, but He gave Himself *for* the church. Through Christ's death on the cross, He gave birth to the church and at the same time, He purchased the church by sacrificing Himself. I doubt the husband will be called upon to sacrifice to the extent that Jesus did, but he must be willing to follow the example of Jesus. The go-ahead man must be willing to sacrifice for his wife. He must be willing to give up of himself for his wife. The word sacrifice as it is use in the biblical context means victim. The go-ahead man must be willing to become a victim *for* his wife, not a victim *to* his wife. Likewise, the wife must be willing to become a victim for her husband not a victim to her husband. This is what Christ did; He became a victim for the Church. Paul tells us in Eph.5:25 that Christ gave Himself for the church.

Eph 5:25 *Husbands, love your wives, even as Christ also loved the church, and gave himself for it.*

The most notable factor about love is that love always gives; love is never selfish. If you were to ask someone what the opposite of love is, they would probably say hate, but I believe the opposite of love is selfishness.

Love can be expressed in many ways, but the one way that we all can relate to is through giving and receiving. God expressed his love for mankind thru giving:

John 3:16 *For God so loved the world, that he gave his only begotten Son, that whosoever believeth in him should not perish, but have everlasting life.*

Every man has the ability to be a go-ahead man; all he needs is himself. Notice what Christ gave to the church—it was Himself. No one can say they do not have anything to give because we all have ourselves. God does not base success in marriage on material things. Money, nice cars, and the big house on the hill are all nice things that may at some point in the marriage are helpful, but the main thing is being willing to give yourself. One of the things I love about God's Word is that it levels the playing field; everyone has the same advantage. There is truly no respect of person with God. Giving of ourselves is one of the hardest things to do. Many of us do not mind giving money or things, but we have a problem giving of ourselves, but Christ gave Himself.

Ps 24:1 *The earth is the Lord's, and the fulness thereof; the world, and they that dwell therein.*

Christ could have given anything for the church because He owns everything. He could have given money, houses, or lands, for these are the things we place value in. Christ made the ultimate sacrifice and gave Himself. Likewise, in our marriage, we must give ourselves. Have you ever heard the expression "money can't buy love"? That is so true and I believe that is why God did not use money. God gave us the thing that meant the most to Him—His son. God recognized the value of the church and He paid the price of its value. As a go-ahead man you must recognized the value of the union of marriage and pay the price of its value with yourself.

I used to work in real estate and the first thing I learned was that something is worth what someone will pay for it. So actually, the buyer sets the value of the property.

"The selling price of a piece of property may be one thing, but if buyers will not pay it, it does you no good." What makes you, the church, of such great value is that Jesus set the value of it; He paid the price of himself. You are of great value to Christ, no matter how anyone else sees you.

When we as the church realize how valuable we are to God, then our actions will portray our value. Knowing what I mean to God as a Christian only makes me love Him more. Because I am of value to Him, I know that He will treat me as something valuable, so I have no problem submitting to Him. In the same manner, the go-ahead man sets the value of his marriage, and when the wife sees the value that her husband places on her and the marriage, she will have no problem submitting to him. Realizing your self-worth will affect how you think and the decisions you make, thereby changing your outcome. We know from Eph 5:25 that Christ gave Himself for the church, but what does that mean and how do that compare to our marriages? Let look at the church. We have learned that the church is made up of the born-again believers. Every Christian is part of the church. Christ gave Himself for us all, not for any one individual's desire. This also helps us understand why we must have a kingdom mentality and focus on kingdom work because that is what Christ gave Himself for.

Likewise, the go-ahead man gives himself to the union of marriage. The go-ahead man knows what God said about the union of marriage, and he is committed to obeying the Word concerning the marriage. He may not always fulfill all of his wife's desires, but he will keep God's Word. Just as we as part of the church at times may desire something that is not healthy for the church as a whole, it is then we must remember that Christ gave Himself for the church.

Scriptures Chapter VII

Matt 19:6 *Wherefore they are no more twain, but one flesh. What therefore God hath joined together, let not man put asunder.*

Phil 4:13 *I can do all things through Christ which strengtheneth me.*

John 15:5 *I am the vine, ye are the branches: He that abideth in me, and I in him, the same bringeth forth much fruit: for without me ye can do nothing.*

Heb 1:13 *But to which of the angels said he at any time, Sit on my right hand, until I make thine enemies thy footstool?*

Rom 8:38-39 *For I am persuaded, that neither death, nor life, nor angels, nor principalities, nor powers, nor things present, nor things to come,39 Nor height, nor depth, nor any other creature, shall be able to separate us from the love of God, which is in Christ Jesus our Lord.*

Am 3:3 *Can two walk together, except they be agreed?*

Matt 18:18-20 *Verily I say unto you, Whatsoever ye shall bind on earth shall be bound in heaven: and whatsoever ye shall loose on earth shall be loosed in heaven.19 Again I say unto you, That if two of you shall agree on earth as touching any thing that they shall ask, it shall be done for them of my Father which is in heaven.20 For where two or three are gathered together in my name, there am I in the midst of them.*

Eph 5:25 *Husbands, love your wives, even as Christ also loved the church, and gave himself for it;*

John 3:16 *For God so loved the world, that he gave his only begotten Son, that whosoever believeth in him should not perish, but have everlasting life.*

Ps 24:1 *The earth is the Lord's, and the fulness thereof; the world, and they that dwell therein.*

CHAPTER VIII

HUSBAND IS THE HEAD OF THE WIFE
CHRIST IS THE HEAD OF THE CHURCH

Eph 5:23 For the husband is the head of the wife, even as Christ is the head of the church: and he is the saviour of the body.

Hos 4:6 My people are destroyed for lack of knowledge: because thou hast rejected knowledge, I will also reject thee, that thou shalt be no priest to me: seeing thou hast forgotten the law of thy God, I will also forget thy children.

Most marriages, including Christian marriages, are destroyed because neither the husband nor the wife understands their roles in the marriage. I find it helpful to look at marriage as an institution that has been set up and ordained by God. Once we are able to recognize marriage as an institution, then we will begin to realize that there are certain roles and responsibilities that the man and the woman fulfill. Let's look at the role of the man: "The husband is the head of the wife." As we analyze this statement, we must ask ourselves three questions: what does it mean to be the head, what is the role of the head, and how should the head conduct himself? These are all great questions, and to answer them we must go to the source, the Word of God. Let take a look at what Jesus said about the head.

Matt. 20:27 *And whosoever will be chief among you, let him be your servant.*

Matt 23:11 *But he that is greatest among you shall be your servant.*

Mark 9:35 *And he sat down, and called the twelve, and saith unto them, If any man desire to be first, the same shall be last of all, and servant of all.*

Not Ladies First But Husbands First

As we look at Jesus' description of head, we see that it is clearly the role of servant. This biblical description of head is totally the opposite of what we have been exposed to in the world's system. We have mistakenly understood the head to mean being in charge and having others serve us. Too often, the husband attempts to dominate the wife. Being the head means the husband is a servant to those under his headship. Why did Christ command the head to serve? I believe it is because the head must go ahead, leading by example.

Eph 5:23 *For the husband is the head of the wife, even as Christ is the head of the church: and he is the saviour of the body.*

Being the head means being out in front and taking the lead. Eph. 5:23 also said *"and he is the saviour of the body."* So to be the head is to be the savior of the body. When I relate this to the husband and wife, it means that the husband is the head, so then the wife is the body. But what does it mean to be the savior? The word savior comes from the Greek word σωτήρ which is pronounced *soter* and it means *"to make or keep safe, to save, to deliver or protect."* Notice that the words dominate and rule are not part of the definition.

Gen 3:16 *Unto the woman he said, I will greatly multiply thy sorrow and thy conception; in sorrow thou shalt bring forth children; and thy desire shall be to thy husband, and he shall rule over thee.*

Because of Eve's sin in the garden, she brought a curse on herself and all women that came after her. In essence, God said that the woman or mother would be overly worried about her children, and she would have a desire to rule over her husband, but her husband would rule over her. This statement that God made in Gen. 3:16 was part of the curse that Adam and Eve brought on themselves in the garden. God, being righteous, pronounced judgment on man for his disobedience. But He carried out the sentence through Jesus Christ, so now man is free from the curse. Thank God for Jesus.

Gal 3:10-13 *For as many as are of the works of the law are under the curse: for it is written, Cursed is every one that continueth not in all things which are written in the book of the law to do them.11 But that no man is justified by the law in the sight of God, it is evident: for, The just shall live by faith. 12 And the law is not of faith: but, The man that doeth them shall live in them.13 Christ hath redeemed us from the curse of the law, being made a curse for us: for it is written, Cursed is every one that hangeth on a tree.*

Go-Ahead "Head"

When you walk into a room, usually the first thing you do is stick your head in the room. One of the main reasons you stick your head in the room first is because your head contains what is needed to determine whether you should bring your whole body into the room. Your head has eyes, which allow you to picture images that may be in the room. Your head has ears, which allow you to pick up sounds that are in the room. Your head has a brain, which allows you to process the images your eyes pick up and the sounds your ears hear. Your brain then takes this information and makes a decision on whether or not it is safe to bring the rest of your body into the room. If the head thinks that the eyes and the ears did not obtain enough information to make a decision, then the head may take a second look, or the mouth may ask for more information. This process is something we do without even thinking about it. Can you imagine if all of our body parts could talk, and your body found itself in danger? Who do you suppose your body parts would blame? Yes, you guessed right, "the head." This is what Jesus meant when He said the head must be a servant to all, meaning the head is responsible to, and responsible for, all of the body.

Most people look to the head, or the leaders, to solve problems, and rightfully so. We feel a company or organization is only as good as it leaders and this holds some truth, but not total truth. An organization's ability to function well will be determined by how well the head and body work together; this is the reason Jesus is so big on agreement.

Am 3:3 *Can two walk together, except they be agreed?*

In a well and healthy body, the members of the body do not refuse to do what the head ask it to do. Your body knows that your head is going to make decisions that are good for the body as a whole. In a Christian marriage, we must adopt the same way of thinking, which is that the head (husband) is only going to make decisions that are good for the marriage as a whole. The number one problem in marriages is the lack of trust between the husband and the wife. The wife does not trust the husband's decisions. The husband does not trust the wife's decisions. The reason that there is a lack of trust is because both the husband and the wife feel that the decisions being made are not in their best interest. We must learn to look at marriage as a whole.

You're Wrong and I'm Right

It has been traditionally taught that women are more spiritual than men. This is simply not true. Women are more emotional and heartfelt than men, which is not a bad thing. But just like any other God given gift, if we are not careful it can get us into trouble. Notice what Paul said:

1Tim 2:14 And Adam was not deceived, but the woman being deceived was in the transgression.

This Scripture by no means releases the man of his part in the fall in the Garden of Eden, but in fact it establishes the man's part. The text said the woman was deceived, meaning Satan tricked her, but Adam was not deceived; he knew he was doing wrong and did it anyway. This is why when we think of man's fall we automatically think of Adam and his willful sin.

Just as the husband is the head of the wife, likewise Christ is the head of the church. Christ is in heaven interceding for the church, but He needs his body to accomplish anything on this earth. Christ needs His body in the earth, the church, to get things done. The church is His hands and His feet in the earth. Christ has the eyes, so He can see what is happening in the earth, and He can see what is going to happen in the earth, but He needs his body the church to take action. That's why obeying God is so important.

Note how your head sends messages to your body and your body obeys and does what your head says. If your body started to do things without your head telling it to, that would mean you were sick. Christ sends messages to the church and the church is supposed to obey. The church must be on the same accord as God so that it can carry out what God said. This is why the man needs his wife, because it doesn't matter what kind of vision the head has if he doesn't have a body to carry it out. Note the Bible says:

Eph 5:22 *Wives, submit yourselves unto your own husbands, as unto the Lord.*

Note that the Bible says that the women should submit to her husband as she submits to the Lord. This means that the husband must be in the same position as the Lord, so when the woman submits to the Lord, at the same time she will be submitting to her husband. This is the main reason that Paul said:

2 Cor 6:14 *Be ye not unequally yoked together with unbelievers: for what fellowship hath righteousness with unrighteousness? and what communion hath light with darkness?*

Even through the husband is the head, he must look to the body to accomplish anything. As the head, the husband can see (eyes), the husband can hear things (ears), he can speak (mouth). These are the functions in the spiritual realm and they require an equally responding physical action. Look at how James puts it:

James 1:22 *But be ye doers of the word, and not hearers only, deceiving your own selves.*

James makes it very clear that if we think we are going to get results simply by hearing the Word but not doing the Word, we are deceiving ourselves. In the same manner, many husbands (the head) deceive themselves when they think they can get along better without their wives (the body). To operate in the physical ream, you need a physical body. As the head with vision, it is the husband's responsibility to instruct and to take the go-ahead to his wife. This is why the traditional marriage vows ask the wife to obey the husband, because faith without works is dead. Women are generally more organized and task oriented than men. This means that once they know what has to be done, they know how to get it done.

Believe the Word

Almost all Christians know that the Bible says the man is the head of the wife. The misunderstanding of this statement has caused a lot of break-ups in marriages, including Christian marriages. Why does this statement, which came straight from the Bible, cause so many problems? The answer is unbelief. The first thing we must learn as Christians is to believe the Word of God. The man is the head of the woman because God created him ahead of the woman. In other words, the man was in the garden first. The man is not the head because he is smarter, stronger, or because he is such a great provider. He is simply the head because that's what the Word of God says. Too often the man does not look like the head or act like the head, so therefore his wife does not recognize him as the head. Herein lays the problem. We must learn to agree with what God said, whether we like it or not. Have you ever had a boss on a job, and you felt he didn't know what he was doing? Yes, it made things harder, but you found a way to work it out, because you recognized him as the boss, and you wanted to keep your job.

In most marriages, the wife has a big problem believing her husband is the head. The reason is that when she physically looks at him, he doesn't look like the head, and he certainly is not acting like the head, and maybe he is not providing like the head. So what do you do then? Well, that's an easy question to answer. Let's ask it like this; what do you do when what the Word of God says and what you see don't match?

2 Cor 5:7 For we walk by faith, not by sight.

When what we see does not match what God's Word says, we only have two choices—we can believe what we see, or we can believe what God's Word says. Let's look at it from another angle. If you are saved, you may not look like what some believers think a saved person should look like. And at times you may not feel like you are saved. You certainly don't always act like you are saved. But through faith, you believe are you saved and that helps you get back on track.

Eph 2:8 For by grace are ye saved through faith; and that not of yourselves: it is the gift of God.

Likewise, the man is not the head because of his behavior but because of what God says!

This problem of unbelief is also shared by the man. The man is looking at himself and what he sees is not matching what the Word of God says the head should be, so he struggles with his headship. Many times the husband does not believe the Word of God that said the husband is the head. The husband at times is not looked at by his wife as the head, therefore he feels he must prove to himself and his wife that he is the head. This way of thinking will cause great problems in a marriage.

I'll Show You

Let's say you were accused and charged with a crime and you said, "I am not guilty. I didn't commit this crime," and your accuser said, "Yes, you did." If you don't change your thinking and agree with your accuser (submit), then proof must come into the picture because there is a question of whether or not you have committed this criminal act.

This is the way of thinking that has entered into our marriages. The Bible declares the husband is the head, but the husband displays unbelief because he is looking at what he is producing in the physical world, and it doesn't look like he is the head. So the husband questions whether are not he is the head. If he doesn't change his way of thinking and submit to the Word of God and just believe he is the head, then he feels he must provide physical proof to show himself and others that he is the head.

In order for the husband and the wife to have success in marriage, it is a matter of accepting their roles in the institution of God's marriage. The Word of God must be the foundation on which the marriage is built. The reason the Word of God is the foundation on which the marriage stands is because the Word is true and it will never change. This is important because if the husband or wife should get upset with each other, it should not disrupt the foundation of the marriage union, thereby enabling the marriage to stand. The foundation of the marriage is not based on feelings, but the Word of God.

This is the same line of thinking that we (the church) should have in our relationship with Christ. What Christ said about the church (me), I believe, not because I see it come to pass, or because I feel it, but because Christ said it and I just believe it. God's Word must be the foundation in our relationship with Him. The reason the Word of God MUST be the foundation in our relationship with Him is because the Word is true, and it will never change. This is important because, if I don't get something I think I should have gotten, or something doesn't go my way, it will not disrupt the foundation of my relationship with God. I will be able to continue to stand on God's Word because the foundation of the relationship is not what I get, but what the Word of God said.

This is one of the things I love about the Word of God; it takes all the pressure off of me and the only thing that is required of me is that I believe it. What we believe as a church is so important because what we believe will determine how we think. Why is it important how we think? Because:

Prov 23:7 *For as he thinketh in his heart, so is he: Eat and drink, saith he to thee; but his heart is not with thee.*

We can clearly see from the Word that if we want to change, we must first change how we think. And to change how we think, we must change what we are hearing. When we change what we are hearing, we will change what we believe. And when we change what we believe, we will change how we think:

Rom 10:17 *So then faith cometh by hearing, and hearing by the word of God.*

SCRIPTURES CHAPTER VIII

Eph 5:23 *For the husband is the head of the wife, even as Christ is the head of the church: and he is the saviour of the body.*

Hos 4:6 *My people are destroyed for lack of knowledge: because thou hast rejected knowledge, I will also reject thee, that thou shalt be no priest to me: seeing thou hast forgotten the law of thy God, I will also forget thy children.*

Matt 20:27 *And whosoever will be chief among you, let him be your servant.*

Matt 23:11 *But he that is greatest among you shall be your servant.*

Mark 9:35 *And he sat down, and called the twelve, and saith unto them, If any man desire to be first, the same shall be last of all, and servant of all.*

Gen 3:16 *Unto the woman he said, I will greatly multiply thy sorrow and thy conception; in sorrow thou shalt bring forth children; and thy desire shall be to thy husband, and he shall rule over thee.*

Gal 3:10-13 *For as many as are of the works of the law are under the curse: for it is written, Cursed is every one that continueth not in all things which are written in the book of the law to do them.11 But that no man is justified by the law in the sight of God, it is evident: for, The just shall live by faith.12 And the law is not of faith: but, The man that doeth them shall live in them.13 Christ hath redeemed us from the curse of the law, being made a curse for us: for it is written, Cursed is every one that hangeth on a tree.*

Am 3:3 *Can two walk together, except they be agreed?*

1 Tim 2:14 *And Adam was not deceived, but the woman being deceived was in the transgression.*

Eph 5:22 *Wives, submit yourselves unto your own husbands, as unto the Lord.*

2 Cor 6:14 *Be ye not unequally yoked together with unbelievers: for what fellowship hath righteousness with unrighteousness? and what communion hath light with darkness?*

James 1:22 *But be ye doers of the word, and not hearers only, deceiving your own selves.*

2 Cor 5:7 *For we walk by faith, not by sight.*

Eph 2:8 *For by grace are ye saved through faith; and that not of yourselves: it is the gift of God.*

Prov 23:7 *For as he thinketh in his heart, so is he: Eat and drink, saith he to thee; but his heart is not with thee.*

Rom 10:17 *So then faith cometh by hearing, and hearing by the word of God.*

CHAPTER IX

WIVES BE SUBJECT TO THEIR HUSBANDS CHURCH BE SUBJECT TO CHRIST

Here we find another parallel between Christ and the church, and the husband and the wife. Just as the church is subject to Christ, the wife is subject to the husband. Let's look at what it means to be subject to someone. The word subject means *"to arrange in an orderly manner."* The first thing we understand is that there is order in subjection. God is a God of order. The Bible teaches us:

1 Cor 14:40 Let all things be done decently and in order.

As we look around in this world, it may seems like the world is full of chaos, but we can notice that the things that God set in the earth are still in order. Every twenty-four hours, the sun sets. It has been that way since God created the world. It doesn't change; you can count on it. This is one of the ways we learn to trust God, because He is predictable, and we know what He is going to do. You would find it hard to trust someone if you didn't know what they were going to do one moment to the next. Sometimes in our life it may seems to us like everything is out of control, but when we allow Christ into our situation, He brings order. Order is important because it keeps us on task. If we do not stay on task, we will find ourselves sidetracked, and we will be doing things that do not promote God's kingdom. Because subjection requires order, we know that it must be voluntary.

God has given us a free will; therefore He will not force us to do anything. This is why the Bible said that though He stands at the door and knocks, He will not force his way in.

Rev 3:20 *Behold, I stand at the door, and knock: if any man hear my voice, and open the door, I will come in to him, and will sup with him, and he with me.*

Anything that we do for God that we expect to be rewarded for, it must be voluntary and out of love. Let's look again at how Paul put it:

Eph 5:24 *Therefore as the church is subject unto Christ, so let the wives be to their own husbands in every thing.*

Notice that Paul said the church is subject to Christ. This tells us that when we become part of the church, we are part of a body that is subject to Christ. When we became a part of Christ's body, we must willingly submit and be subject to His authority. Look at how Jesus put it John 15:

John 15:2-6 *Every branch in me that beareth not fruit he taketh away: and every branch that beareth fruit, he purgeth it, that it may bring forth more fruit.3 Now ye are clean through the word which I have spoken* *unto you. 4 Abide in me, and I in you. As the branch cannot bear fruit of itself, except it abide in the vine; no more can ye, except ye abide in me. 5 I am the vine, ye are the branches: He that abideth in me, and I in him, the same bringeth forth much fruit: for without me ye can do nothing. 6 If a man abide not in me, he is cast forth as a branch, and is withered; and men gather them, and cast them into the fire, and they are burned.*

God has already established rules and guidelines for His church. God will not force us to join His church, but we must understand that the guidelines for the church were set before we decided to join it. Paul encourages us in Eph 5:24, saying: *Therefore as the church is subject unto Christ, so let the wives be to their own husbands in every thing.* Eph.5:24a says "is," meaning present, when making references to the church, but Eph.5:24b says "let," meaning "allow," when referring to what the wife should do.

God shows unconditional love to his church, and God wants a voluntary response of subjection from us. When we voluntarily subject ourselves to Christ, we can expect Christ to take care of us. When we belong to Christ, we are part of His body, and we are subject to Him, so we obey Him. Look at what Jesus said in Luke:

Luke 6:46 *And why call ye me, Lord, Lord, and do not the things which I say?*

Notice Jesus said they called Him "Lord, Lord," but they would not obey Him. They recognized His authority, but they would not be subject to Him. Just as the members of our body obey the messages our brain sends it, we as members of Christ's body must obey the messages He gives us. If we do not obey God, we cannot expect the results that the Bible teaches we should have. What would you think of a man that worked and got paid and would not take care of his family? Look what Paul said:

1 Tim 5:8 But if any provide not for his own, and specially for those of his own house, he hath denied the faith, and is worse than an infidel.

We know from this Scripture that if we are part of His church, we belong to Him. Since we belong to God, we can expect Him to protect and provide for us.

Another definition for "subject" that I find interesting is *"to put under, place (beneath)."* This means that to subject yourself to someone, you must be placed under their authority or power. From this definition we understand that the authority and power is there first, then we place ourselves under that authority and power. Being under the authority and power of someone can be trying until we come to understand that all authority and power come from God.

Rom 13:1 Let every soul be subject unto the higher powers. For there is no power but of God: the powers that be are ordained of God.

Christ is the head of the church whether or not we subject ourselves to His power and authority or not. The husband is the head of the wife whether she be subject to his power and authority or not. The thing we must understand about God is that what God said in His Word is true. If no one in the world believed it, it would still be true. If no one in the world did it, it would still true. Too often the wife will come up short in the marriage because she does not utilize the authority and power that she has at her disposal. God has declared that the two are one, so what the husband possesses so does the wife. Some wives do not even recognize their husband's authority and power let alone allow themselves to be subject to it.

Prov 14:1 *Every wise woman buildeth her house: but the foolish plucketh it down with her hands.*

Being wise is not necessary being smart or having a lot of knowledge. It is simply utilizing well what you have available to you.

He's Got You Covered?

As we understand that "subject" means "*put under, place (beneath)*," we can see that as the wife is subject to her husband, the husband is her covering. This covering that the husband provides to his wife is another function of his headship. For the husband to cover his wife means he is her protector; he covers her weaknesses and her shortcomings. In other words, he loves her. This is what the Scripture means in:

1 Peter 4:8 *And above all things have fervent charity among yourselves: for charity shall cover the multitude of sins.*

A go-ahead man will never belittle, embarrass, or tear his wife down. He understands that whatever he does to his wife, he does to himself. A go-ahead man will always encourage and push his wife to be all that she can be and all that God has called her to be, just as Christ encourages us to do.

Phil 3:13-14 *Brethren, I count not myself to have apprehended: but this one thing I do, forgetting those things which are behind, and reaching forth unto those things which are before,14 I press toward the mark for the prize of the high calling of God in Christ Jesus.*

Just as we, the church, place ourselves under the authority and power of Christ, likewise, the wife places herself under the authority of the husband. The wife traditionally takes the husband's name. Christ has given us His name, which represents his authority and power.

John 14:14 *If ye shall ask any thing in my name, I will do it.*

Mark 16:17 *And these signs shall follow them that believe; In my name shall they cast out devils; they shall speak with new tongues.*

John 15:16 *Ye have not chosen me, but I have chosen you, and ordained you, that ye should go and bring forth fruit, and that your fruit should remain: that whatsoever ye shall ask of the Father in my name, he may give it you.*

Because Christ is the head of the church, the authority and power that we are allowed to use is on Christ's behalf. This is why it is so important that we be in agreement with God. As the body of Christ, we work with

Christ, carrying out His instructions on earth; I guess you could say we are his helpmeet! Christ is also our covering; He is our protector.

Matt 28:20 *Teaching them to observe all things whatsoever I have commanded you: and, lo, I am with you alway, even unto the end of the world. Amen.*

Likewise, the husband is the wife's covering, and he is also her protector. Because the husband and the wife are one, when you see one, you see the other. Just as the husband encourages and builds up his wife, Christ encourages and builds up His church.

Matt 5:13-16 *Ye are the salt of the earth: but if the salt have lost his savour, wherewith shall it be salted? it is thenceforth good for nothing, but to be cast out, and to be trodden under foot of men.14 Ye are the light of the world. A city that is set on an hill cannot be hid.15 Neither do men light a candle, and put it under a bushel, but on a candlestick; and it giveth light unto all that are in the house.16 Let your light so shine before men, that they may see your good works, and glorify your Father which is in heaven.*

The go-ahead man will always show appreciation and encourage his wife; he will recognize her for the jewel that she is. A go-ahead man understands that he has something more precious than rubies.

Prov 31:10-31 *Who can find a virtuous woman? for her price is far above rubies.11 The heart of her husband doth safely trust in her, so that he shall have no need of spoil.12 She will do him good and not evil all the days of her life.13 She seeketh wool, and flax, and worketh willingly with her* *hands.14 She is like the merchants' ships; she bringeth her food from afar.15 She riseth also while it is yet night, and giveth meat to her household, and a portion to her maidens.16 She considereth a field, and buyeth it: with the fruit of her hands she planteth a vineyard.17 She girdeth her loins with strength, and strengtheneth her arms.18 She perceiveth that her merchandise is good: her candle goeth not out by night.19 She layeth her hands to the spindle, and her hands hold the distaff.20 She stretcheth out her hand to the poor; yea, she reacheth forth her hands to the needy.21 She is not afraid of the snow for her household: for all her household are clothed with scarlet.22 She maketh herself coverings of tapestry; her clothing is silk and purple.23 Her husband is known in the gates, when he sitteth among the elders of the land.24 She maketh fine linen, and selleth it; and delivereth girdles unto the merchant.25 Strength and honour are her clothing; and she shall rejoice in time to come.26 She openeth her mouth with wisdom; and in her tongue is the law of kindness.27 She looketh well to the ways of her household, and eateth not the bread of idleness.28 Her children arise up, and call her blessed; her husband also, and he praiseth her.29 Many daughters have done virtuously, but thou excellest them all.30 Favour is deceitful, and beauty is vain: but a woman that feareth the Lord, she shall be praised.31 Give her of the fruit of her hands; and let her own works praise her in the gates.*

The Purpose of the Church

God's purpose has not changed since the Garden of Eden. As I carefully studied the Scriptures, I found one consonant thing about God in His Word. No matter how God reveals Himself in the Bible, His love for man and His desire to live among men comes through. All God ever wanted was to be back in fellowship with man. That is what the sacrificial system of the Old Testament was all about, God finding a way to come down and spend time with man. Jesus finished the work that God started when He became the sacrifice on the cross.

The Church is the fulfillment of God's plan; it is how He lives among men. We the church are the body of Christ in the earth, and our job is to glorify the Father. In Matt 5:16, Jesus tells us that the reason we let our light shine is to glorify the Father in heaven. Jesus wants the Father to be glorified. This example teaches us that our works on this earth are to be unselfish. I believe too often we take things too personally, especially our failures. We must learn not to take our failures personally and neither our successes. God taught me a long time ago that if I blamed myself every time I failed, then I would take credit every time I succeeded. Christ being our covering shows us what we should expect; He does not leave us helpless and without warning.

Luke 21:17 *And ye shall be hated of all men for my name's sake.*

Matt 10:16-17 *Behold, I send you forth as sheep in the midst of wolves: be ye therefore wise as serpents, and harmless as doves.17 But beware of men: for they will deliver you up to the councils, and they will scourge you in their synagogues.*

Likewise the go-ahead man understands that everything that his wife does weather she fails or succeeds reflect on him as well as her, so he encourages and builds her up, because they are in it together. He will never leave or forsake her, until death do they part.

SCRIPTURES CHAPTER IX

1 Cor 14:40 *Let all things be done decently and in order.*

Rev 3:20 *Behold, I stand at the door, and knock: if any man hear my voice, and open the door, I will come in to him, and will sup with him, and he with me.*

Eph 5:24 *Therefore as the church is subject unto Christ, so let the wives be to their own husbands in every thing.*

John 15:2-6 *Every branch in me that beareth not fruit he taketh away: and every branch that beareth fruit, he purgeth it, that it may bring forth more fruit.3 Now ye are clean through the word which I have spoken unto you.4 Abide in me, and I in you. As the branch cannot bear fruit of itself, except it abide in the vine; no more can ye, except ye abide in me.5 I am the vine, ye are the branches: He that abideth in me, and I in him, the same bringeth forth much fruit: for without me ye can do nothing.6 If a man abide not in me, he is cast forth as a branch, and is withered; and men gather them, and cast them into the fire, and they are burned.*

Luke 6:46 *And why call ye me, Lord, Lord, and do not the things which I say?*

1 Tim 5:8 *But if any provide not for his own, and specially for those of his own house, he hath denied the faith, and is worse than an infidel.*

Rom 13:1 *Let every soul be subject unto the higher powers. For there is no power but of God: the powers that be are ordained of God.*

Prov 14:1 *Every wise woman buildeth her house: but the foolish plucketh it down with her hands.*

1 Peter 4:8 *And above all things have fervent charity among yourselves: for charity shall cover the multitude of sins.*

Phil 3:13-14 *Brethren, I count not myself to have apprehended: but this one thing I do, forgetting those things which are behind, and reaching forth unto those things which are before,14 I press toward the mark for the prize of the high calling of God in Christ Jesus.*

John 14:14 *If ye shall ask any thing in my name, I will do it.*

Mark 16:17 *And these signs shall follow them that believe; In my name shall they cast out devils; they shall speak with new tongues.*

John 15:16 *Ye have not chosen me, but I have chosen you, and ordained you, that ye should go and bring forth fruit, and that your fruit should remain: that whatsoever ye shall ask of the Father in my name, he may give it you.*

Matt 28:20 *Teaching them to observe all things whatsoever I have commanded you: and, lo, I am with you alway, even unto the end of the world. Amen.*

Matt 5:13-16 *Ye are the salt of the earth: but if the salt have lost his savour, wherewith shall it be salted? it is thenceforth good for nothing, but to be cast out, and to be trodden under foot of men.14 Ye are the light of the world. A city that is set on an hill cannot be hid.15 Neither do men light a candle, and put it under a bushel, but on a candlestick; and it giveth light unto all that are in the house.16 Let your light so shine before men, that they may see your good works, and glorify your Father which is in heaven.*

Prov 31:10-31 *Who can find a virtuous woman? for her price is far above rubies.11 The heart of her husband doth safely trust in her, so that he shall have no need of spoil.12 She will do him good and not evil all the days of her life.13 She seeketh wool, and flax, and worketh willingly with her hands.14 She is like the merchants' ships; she bringeth her food from afar.15 She riseth also while it is yet night, and giveth meat to her household, and a portion to her maidens.16 She considereth a field, and buyeth it: with the fruit of her hands she planteth a vineyard.17 She girdeth her loins with strength, and strengtheneth her arms.18 She perceiveth that her merchandise is good: her candle goeth not out by night.19 She layeth her hands to the spindle, and her hands hold the distaff.20 She stretcheth out her hand to the poor; yea, she reacheth forth her hands to the needy.21 She is not afraid of the snow for her household: for all her household are clothed with scarlet.22 She maketh herself coverings of tapestry; her clothing is silk and purple.23 Her husband is known in the gates, when he sitteth among the elders of the land.24 She maketh fine linen, and selleth it; and delivereth girdles unto the merchant.25 Strength and honour are her clothing; and she shall rejoice in time to come.26 She openeth her mouth with wisdom; and in her tongue is the law of kindness.27 She looketh well to the ways of her household, and eateth not the bread of idleness.28 Her children arise up, and call her blessed; her husband also, and he praiseth her.29 Many daughters have done virtuously, but thou excellest them all.30 Favour is deceitful, and beauty is vain: but a woman that feareth the Lord, she shall be praised.31 Give her of the fruit of her hands; and let her own works praise her in the gates.*

Luke 21:17 *And ye shall be hated of all men for my name's sake.*

Matt 10:16-17 *Behold, I send you forth as sheep in the midst of wolves: be ye therefore wise as serpents, and harmless as doves.17 But beware of men: for they will deliver you up to the councils, and they will scourge you in their synagogues.*

CHAPTER X

CHRIST SANCTIFIED THE CHURCH
HUSBAND SANCTIFIED THE WIFE

To sanctify means *"to purify by expiation, to make free from the guilt of sin."* Christ sanctified the church, which means He set the church apart. We must ask ourselves why Christ set the church apart. The reason we usually set something apart is because we have a special use for it later. God has always set His people apart. God set the children of Israel apart in the land of Goshen when He brought destruction on Egypt, because He had a special use for them. Before God will use us as a people, He first sets us apart. One of the definitions of the word Holy is *"to be set apart."* Christ has set His church apart because He has a special use for his church; this is why He gave Himself for His church. The special use that Christ has for His church is that the church is suppose to represent God in the earth; this is why the church must be Holy, because God is Holy.

1 Peter 1:16 Because it is written, Be ye holy; for I am holy.

Eph 5:26-27 That he might sanctify and cleanse it with the washing of water by the word, 27 That he might present it to himself a glorious church, not having spot, or wrinkle, or any such thing; but that it should be holy and without blemish.

Christ expected the church to *"be holy and without blemish."* Christ wants to church to be holy (set apart) and without blemish (to look good). These are the expectations that the husband should have for the wife, that she might feel set apart (special) and that she might look good to him.

The go-ahead man will always seek to better his wife, helping her to be all that God has called her to be. The reason the husband seeks to better his wife is the same reason that Christ seeks to make the church Holy and without blemish: Christ presents his church to Himself to represent Him. So likewise the husband presents his wife to himself and she represent Him. The same way that the wife reflects the husband, so the church reflects Christ.

Rev 19:6-8 *And I heard as it were the voice of a great multitude, and as the voice of many waters, and as the voice of mighty thunderings, saying, Alleluia: for the Lord God omnipotent reigneth.7 Let us be glad and rejoice, and give honour to him: for the marriage of the Lamb is come, and his wife hath made herself ready.8 And to her was granted that she should be arrayed in fine linen, clean and white: for the fine linen is the righteousness of saints.*

Notice Christ's progression: He loves the church, He gives Himself for the church, He cleans the church, and He presents it to Himself in marriage. likewise, the husband loves his wife, he gives himself and all that he has to the wife, he dresses her up and makes her look good, and then he presents her to himself in marriage.

A Child of God

If you were to do a study of the Old Testament, you would find that God's people were referred to as Hebrews or Jews. The Hebrews and the Jews are descendants of Abraham, and they made up God's people. Under the New Testament Covenant, it is the church that makes up God's people. As we said earlier, signing your name on the roll doesn't make you part of God's church; nor does coming to church every Sunday or paying tithes. Becoming part of God's church in the New Testament follows the same process it took in the Old Testament: to become part of God's people, you had to be born into it.

In the Old Testament, to be part of God's people you had to be a descendant of Abraham. Likewise, to be a part of God's church you must be a descendant of Christ. How do you become a descendant of Christ? You have already been born, so how can you change your heritage? That is a good question and is the same one that Nicodemus asked in John 3:

John 3:3-7 Jesus answered and said unto him, Verily, verily, I say unto thee, Except a man be born again, he cannot see the kingdom of God. Nicodemus saith unto him, How can a man be born when he is old? can he enter the second time into his mother's womb, and be born?5 Jesus answered, Verily, verily, I say unto thee, Except a man be born of water and of the Spirit, he cannot enter into the kingdom of God.6 That which is born of the flesh is flesh; and that which is born of the Spirit is spirit.7 Marvel not that I said unto thee, Ye must be born again.

To be part of God's church; you must be born into it. Whatever you are born as is who you are; it is your nature. This is why fallen man had to be born again.

For example, if you have a dog, you can dress it up and teach it tricks. You might even teach it how to talk. But it is still a dog, and in the right situation will probably bite because that is the nature of a dog and that's what dogs do.

I Was Born To...

Man in his fallen state is sinful, and what does a sinful man do? He sins; it is his nature. As sinful men with sinful natures, we can do good deeds, and we can do great works. We could even go to church every Sunday and sing in the choir. We might even preach the gospel. But if we have not been born again, we still have that old sin nature and we are not part of Christ's church. This is the reason Christ said to Nicodemus three times that you must be born again:

John 3:3 Jesus answered and said unto him, Verily, verily, I say unto thee, Except <u>a man be born again</u>, he cannot see the kingdom of God.

John 3:5 Jesus answered, Verily, verily, I say unto thee, Except <u>a man be born of water and of the Spirit</u>, he cannot enter into the kingdom of God.

John 3:7 *Marvel not that I said unto thee, Ye <u>must be born again</u>.*

Christ purified the church, His people, by removing impurities from them and making amends for them. We know as Christians that Christ has made us free from sin. Because we are born again through Christ, our sin nature has been changed to a righteous nature!

Rom 6:18 *Being then made free from sin, ye became the servants of righteousness.*

Does that mean we are not ever going to sin again? Of course it doesn't. The sinful man may do good deeds and do a lot of churchy stuff, but that doesn't change his sinful nature. Likewise, if the righteous man mistakenly does bad deeds, that doesn't change his righteous nature. In order for us, the church, to do Christ's will, we must develop a relationship with Christ. Our relationship with Christ, and each other, is how the world will know we belong to Christ, and that we are faithful to Him.

John 13:34-35 *A new commandment I give unto you, That ye love one another; as I have loved you, that ye also love one another. 35 By this shall all men know that ye are my disciples, if ye have love one to another.*

No More Two but One

When the man and the woman get married, in God's eyes they become one. If the husband and the wife have a good relationship, that is a good witness to the unsaved world because the world will look at them and see the same oneness that God sees. The relationship that the husband

and the wife have will allow the world to see that they are faithful to one another and that they are in love. If the husband and the wife have a bad relationship, they are still married and God still sees them as one. The husband being the head and the wife being the body, they must work together; they must have some type of relationship. The better the relationship, the better they work together. If the body and the head are not working together, then they are sick. Also, as people of God, we must develop a relationship with Christ. The better the relationship, the more effective we can be for Christ. In our relationship with God we must learn to express our love to God in a spiritual way because God is a Spirit. Likewise we must express our love to our spouse in a physical way because we are physical. Just as Christ set the church apart for his special use, the husband sets his wife apart for his special use. In the eyes of the husband, his wife is like no other woman, he will do anything for her including dying for her. God gave the husband and the wife a desire to have sexual relation to express their love toward one another in a physical way. The go ahead man recognizes his wife as being special, and nothing is too good for her.

Heb 13:4 *Marriage is honourable in all, and the bed undefiled: but whoremongers and adulterers God will judge.*

God said that marriage is honorable, and as such it is nothing to be taken lightly. God created sex only for marriage and He wants the husband and the wife to enjoy each other sexually. God also put safe guards in place to protect the sexual relationship between the husband and the wife by promising in Heb. 13:4 to judge all sexual activity that takes place outside of marriage. Have you ever noticed that in the bible when God refers to sexual intercourse between the husband and the wife He uses the phase *"he knew her"*, but when he refers to sex between an unmarried man and woman He uses the phase *"he went into her"?* God takes the sexual relationship between the husband and the wife very serious and so should we, we should also remember that sex was and is God's ideal He is the one that started it and He knows how He wants to handle it in fact the frist command that God gave man was to be fruitful and multiply. The bible say in Matt. 5:32 that fornication is the only acceptable reason for divorced.

Matt 5:32 But I say unto you, That whosoever shall put away his wife, saving for the cause of fornication, causeth her to commit adultery: and whosoever shall marry her that is divorced committeth adultery.

God has placed a death penalty on adultery this shows us how God feels about the sanity of the sexual relationship between the husband and the wife.

Lev 20:10 And the man that committeth adultery with another man's wife, even he that committeth adultery with his neighbour's wife, the adulterer and the adulteress shall surely be put to death.

Lev 18:6-19 None of you shall approach to any that is near of kin to him, to uncover their nakedness: I am the Lord. 7 The nakedness of thy father, or the nakedness of thy mother, shalt thou not uncover: she is thy mother; thou shalt not uncover her nakedness. 8 The nakedness of thy father's wife shalt thou not uncover: it is thy father's nakedness. 9 The nakedness of thy sister, the daughter of thy father, or daughter of thy mother, whether she be born at home, or born abroad, even their nakedness thou shalt not uncover.10 The nakedness of thy son's daughter, or of thy daughter's daughter, even their nakedness thou shalt not uncover: for theirs is thine own nakedness.11 The nakedness of thy father's wife's daughter, begotten of thy father, she is thy sister, thou shalt not uncover her nakedness.12 Thou shalt not uncover the nakedness of thy father's sister: she is thy father's near kinswoman.13 Thou shalt not uncover the nakedness of thy mother's sister: for she is thy mother's near kinswoman.14 Thou shalt not uncover the nakedness of thy father's brother, thou shalt not approach to his wife: she is thine aunt.15 Thou shalt not uncover the nakedness of thy daughter in law: she is thy son's wife; thou shalt not uncover her nakedness.16 Thou shalt not uncover the nakedness of thy brother's wife: it is thy brother's nakedness.17 Thou shalt not uncover the nakedness of a woman and her daughter, neither shalt thou take her son's daughter, or her daughter's daughter, to uncover her nakedness; for they are her near kinswomen: it is wickedness.18 Neither shalt thou take a wife to her sister, to vex her, to uncover her nakedness, beside the other in her life time.

SCRIPTURES CHAPTER X

1 Peter 1:16 *Because it is written, Be ye holy; for I am holy.*

Eph 5:26-27 *That he might sanctify and cleanse it with the washing of water by the word, 27 That he might present it to himself a glorious church, not having spot, or wrinkle, or any such thing; but that it should be holy and without blemish.*

Rev 19:6-8 *And I heard as it were the voice of a great multitude, and as the voice of many waters, and as the voice of mighty thunderings, saying, Alleluia: for the Lord God omnipotent reigneth.7 Let us be glad and rejoice, and give honour to him: for the marriage of the Lamb is come, and his wife hath made herself ready.8 And to her was granted that she should be arrayed in fine linen, clean and white: for the fine linen is the righteousness of saints.*

John 3:3-7 *Jesus answered and said unto him, Verily, verily, I say unto thee, Except a man be born again, he cannot see the kingdom of God.4 Nicodemus saith unto him, How can a man be born when he is old? can he enter the second time into his mother's womb, and be born?5 Jesus answered, Verily, verily, I say unto thee, Except a man be born of water and of the Spirit, he cannot enter into the kingdom of God.6 That which is born of the flesh is flesh; and that which is born of the Spirit is spirit.7 Marvel not that I said unto thee, Ye must be born again.*

Rom 6:18 *Being then made free from sin, ye became the servants of righteousness.*

John 13:34-35 *A new commandment I give unto you, That ye love one another; as I have loved you, that ye also love one another.35 By this shall all men know that ye are my disciples, if ye have love one to another.*

Heb 13:4 *Marriage is honourable in all, and the bed undefiled: but whoremongers and adulterers God will judge.*

Matt 5:32 *But I say unto you, That whosoever shall put away his wife, saving for the cause of fornication, causeth her to commit adultery: and whosoever shall marry her that is divorced committeth adultery.*

Lev 20:10 *And the man that committeth adultery with another man's wife, even he that committeth adultery with his neighbour's wife, the adulterer and the adulteress shall surely be put to death.*

Lev 18:6-19 *None of you shall approach to any that is near of kin to him, to uncover their nakedness: I am the Lord. 7 The nakedness of thy father, or the nakedness of thy mother, shalt thou not uncover: she is thy mother; thou shalt not uncover* *her nakedness.8 The nakedness of thy father's wife shalt thou not uncover: it is thy father's nakedness.9 The nakedness of thy sister, the daughter of thy father, or daughter of thy mother, whether she be born at home, or born abroad, even their nakedness thou shalt not uncover.10 The nakedness of thy son's daughter, or of thy daughter's daughter, even their nakedness thou shalt not uncover: for theirs is thine own nakedness.11 The nakedness of thy father's wife's daughter, begotten of thy father, she is thy sister, thou shalt not uncover her nakedness.12 Thou shalt not uncover the nakedness of thy father's sister: she is thy father's near kinswoman.13 Thou shalt not uncover the nakedness of thy mother's sister: for she is thy mother's near kinswoman.14 Thou shalt not uncover the nakedness of thy father's brother, thou shalt not approach to his wife: she is thine aunt.15 Thou shalt not uncover the nakedness of thy daughter in law: she is thy son's wife; thou shalt not uncover her nakedness.16 Thou shalt not uncover the nakedness of thy brother's wife: it is thy brother's nakedness.17 Thou shalt not uncover the nakedness of a woman and her daughter, neither shalt thou take her son's daughter, or her daughter's daughter, to uncover her nakedness; for they are her near kinswomen: it is wickedness.18 Neither shalt thou take a wife to her sister, to vex her, to uncover her nakedness, beside the other in her life time.*

CHAPTER XI

HOW TO BECOME A GO-AHEAD MAN

Eph 6:10-18 Finally, my brethren, be strong in the Lord, and in the power of his might. Put on the whole armour of God, that ye may be able to stand against the wiles of the devil. For we wrestle not against flesh and blood, but against principalities, against powers, against the rulers of the darkness of this world, against spiritual wickedness in high places. Wherefore take unto you the whole armour of God, that ye may be able to withstand in the evil day, and having done all, to stand. Stand therefore, having your loins girt about with truth, and having on the breastplate of righteousness; And your feet shod with the preparation of the gospel of peace; Above all, taking the shield of faith, wherewith ye shall be able to quench all the fiery darts of the wicked. And take the helmet of salvation, and the sword of the Spirit, which is the word of God; Praying always with all prayer and supplication in the Spirit, and watching thereunto with all perseverance and supplication for all saints.

In Eph 6:10-18 the Holy Spirit shows us a perfect path to becoming a go-ahead man. Paul's writing to the church in Ephesus is very interesting because he is writing to gentiles who have recently become Christians. Paul

110

starts this epistle by teaching them that they have been chosen by God. Paul then reminds them who they used to be, and explains that now they are a new creation in Christ. Paul then shows them the revelation of the revealed mystery of the Church. Paul uses this mystery to show them how to treat one another. He then concludes this epistle by letting them know that they are in a war. Once Paul tells them that they are in a war, the first thing he clarifies is that their war was not with each other.

I Have No Beef with You

In becoming a go-ahead man, the most important revelation you can get is the understanding that your war is not with your wife. The enemy would like nothing better than to get you and your spouse at odds with each other. Satan would like both of you to think that the other one is the enemy. One thing that the go-ahead man must get very skillful at, especially when relating to his wife, is recognizing when Satan comes into the conversation. Think about some of the arguments you and your spouse have had. In many of them, one or both of you were accusing the other of something. We understand from the Word of God that Satan is an accuser of the brethren, so we can recognize that sprit as coming from Satan.

Revelation 12:10 *And I heard a loud voice saying in heaven, Now is come salvation, and strength, and the kingdom of our God, and the power of his Christ: for the accuser of our brethren is cast down, which accused them before our God day and night.*

Some people do not even want to acknowledge the very existence of Satan. I am sure Satan would like nothing better than for people to think that he does not exist. In order to have consistent victories over Satan, we must acknowledge him as the real enemy.

Eph 6:10 *Finally, my brethren, be strong in the Lord, and in the power of his might.*

Another way to say this is that God wants us to deal with the enemy in the Lord's power and not our own power. The go-ahead man is simply a man of God, and being a man of God, he must realize that without Christ, he can do nothing. There are times that the husband may forget this, especially if he has a wife and children that admire him and are constantly uplifting him. But don't fool yourselves, husbands. If you are going to be successful, you are going to need the LORD.

Time to Get Dressed

Eph 6:11 *Put on the whole armour of God, that ye may be able to stand against the wiles of the devil.*

What is the armor of God? Simply put, the armor of God is the Word of God. God wants us to understand that we must wear His Word like a soldier wears armor. In the Bible days, if you saw someone in armor, you would know that they were a soldier that belonged to an army. Even if you did not see any more soldiers at the time, you would know they were close by. The go-ahead man does not have to tell people that he is a go-ahead man; people will know it by how the Word of God fits him. The Word of God covers us just like the armor covers the solider. The born -again Christians can be recognized by what they have on.

The armor that Paul is speaking about is full body armor. With this armor on, the solider could not be recognized because his face was also covered with armor, but by looking at his armor, you knew he was a soldier. If the soldier face was showing, that meant he did not have on all of his armor. This is what Paul means by putting on the whole armor of God. Paul tells us why we are to put on this armor: *"That ye may be able to stand against the wiles of the devil."*

The armor is to protect us while we stand. If you have ever been to a professional fight, you have seen that the winner is usually determined by who is left standing. The armor in itself will enable you to continue to stand. Standing means we never give up. In the marriage relationship, things will get hard at times, but we must continue to stand. We will never be able to stand on our own power; this is why the go-ahead man always wears the armor of God and stands in the power of the Lord. Putting on the armor of God means I am doing what God's Word says to do. Doing God's Word may not turn many heads on the earth, but the spirit world certainly takes notice and that is where the real fight is!

Ready to Fight?

The fight is not against flesh and blood. In other words, the fight is not against a human man. We don't need to think too hard to figure out that if the fight is not against flesh and blood, then it must be against a

113

spirit. Because our fight is against a spirit, we need spiritual weapons, such as the Word of God.

John 6:63 *It is the spirit that quickeneth; the flesh profiteth nothing: the words that I speak unto you, they are spirit, and they are life.*

The entire spirit world responds to the Word of God. We as God's creation do not magnify God's Word in the earth like we should, and since we don't, God's Word is not highly looked upon in the earth. This is not so in the spirit world. Understanding how things are done in the spirit world is how we gain victory in our lives in the physical world. Paul tells us we are fighting *"against principalities."* The word "principalities" in the Greek is (ἀρχή) and comes from the word "prince," which means *"first."* This word (ἀρχή) is used fifty-five times in the New Testament, and over forty of those times it is translated as "beginning or beginnings." You might ask, "What does that mean?" That means that your problems did not start with your spouse when you got married, although it may seem that way sometimes. All of the troubles in the world began in the Garden of Eden. We must realize that our troubles do not originate with people, but people can put us in a position where we must face what has been there from the beginning. Let's look at what Jesus said about Satan in reference to the beginning:

John 8:44 *Ye are of your father the devil, and the lusts of your father ye will do. He was a murderer from the beginning, and abode not in the truth, because there is no truth in him. When he speaketh a lie, he speaketh of his own: for he is a liar, and the father of it.*

Paul tells us something else about what we are fighting against by using the word "powers." The Greek word is *"exousia"* and it means *"power of choice, liberty of doing as one pleases."* That is what gets us into trouble most of the time, doing what pleases us. The struggle that we have is with our mind, because our minds may tell us one thing while the Word of God tells us something else. It is the power of choice that makes me wrestle in my mind, not my spouse.

I Can't Change You

To be a successful go-ahead man, you must remember that you can only be responsible for your behavior and no one else's. Paul shows us that we are fighting against *"the rulers of the darkness of this world."* Here, Paul brings the fight closer to home. He uses the term *"of this world,"* which means that something is going on now, in this world, that is causing me a problem. Paul is talking here about how demonic influences are influencing our rulers, lawmakers, and people in high-powered positions. God's position is that if the people that make the laws of the land are in darkness, then they are going to make laws that do not reflect God's values, which in turn affects us as Christians. For this very reason, Paul left instructions with Timothy:

1 Tim 2:1-2 I exhort therefore, that, first of all, supplications, prayers, Intercessions, and giving of thanks, be made for all men;2 For kings, and for all that are in authority; that we may lead a quiet and peaceable life in all godliness and honesty.

This struggle with the *"rulers of the darkness of this world"* is against a system, not flesh and blood. Paul tells us also that we are fighting *"against spiritual wickedness in high places."* The Scripture lets us know here that we not only struggle with influences from this world's system, but we also struggle with satanic influences. But Satan can only influence our minds, not our actions. We have the power to carry out his suggestions or not. This is a big problem in relationships because our mind can tells us some crazy things at times.

How Can I Win?

Paul begins to tell us how we are going to win:

Eph 6:13 Wherefore take unto you the whole armour of God, that ye may be able to withstand in the evil day, and having done all, to stand.

Again, Paul tells us to stand. Standing is very important in anything that we do for God. The reason standing is a priority is that God has already won the battle for us; we just need to continue to stand until we can see the manifestation of the victory in our life.

1 Cor 15:57-58 But thanks be to God, which giveth us the victory through our Lord Jesus Christ.58 Therefore, my beloved brethren, be ye stedfast, unmoveable, always abounding in the work of the Lord, forasmuch as ye know that your labour is not in vain in the Lord.

Look at what the Scripture says in 1 Cor 15:57: *"God giveth us the victory."* Notice that God gives us the victory not the battle! Also in 1 Cor 15:58, the text says that since God has given us the victory, we need to be steadfast and unmovable. It goes on to say that we should *"abound or stand"* in the work that the Lord has done; when we do that, we will know that our *"labour or standing"* is not in vain. Standing sounds easy, but if you have ever really stood on the Word of God, you know that it can get very hard at times. The reason standing is so hard is because your circumstances may not look like what the Word of God say but remember, you are not standing on circumstances; you are standing on the Word of God. You may even look like a fool at times while you stand on the Word of God. Even with mountains of evidence that say, "that is not going to work," keep on standing.

Just as God has left us instructions on how to do everything that we will need to do, He has also let us instructions on how to stand. God tells us to *"Stand therefore, having your loins girt about with truth."* The text lets us know here that we must stand on the truth, and the truth is the Word of God. Christians must always take a stand on what the Word of God says because we know that God will always perform His Word. The go-ahead man understands that it is not his responsibility to bring God's Word to pass; he just has to obey it.

Don't Forget Your Belt

The Holy Spirit references the truth in Eph. 6:14 as a belt. I believe that the Holy Spirit uses the belt here because a belt is what holds our clothes in place. Have you ever seen the young kids that have their pants hanging down? It is because they do not have their belt in the right place. Everything that we believe about the Word is truth; truth is what holds everything else in place.

Paul said we must also *"have on the breastplate of righteousness."* The Christian must learn to wear their righteousness like a breastplate. I believe that the greatest struggle that most Christians have is to not believe they are righteous. The reason we struggle with this is because we think that our righteousness is based on us and what we do, and we know that we have not done everything right. We must understand that we are not righteous because we do everything right; we are righteous because the Word of God says so.

Rom 3:21-24 But now the righteousness of God without the law is manifested, being witnessed by the law and the prophets; 22 Even the righteousness of God which is by faith of Jesus Christ unto all and upon all them that believe: for there is no difference: 23 For all have sinned, and come short of the glory of God.

Have you ever noticed how the enemy always points you to your shortcomings or the things you have done wrong? The reason the enemy does this is because he does not want you to display your righteousness. When Christians realizes that they are righteous, it boosts their faith and their confidence and it makes it much harder for the enemy to defeat them and keep them from standing.

Do I Need Shoes?

Our feet play a big part in our standing. Paul said we should have our *"feet shod with the preparation of the gospel of peace."* The Bible tells us in Eph. 6:15 that as we stand, we are to be prepared with the gospel of peace. What does this mean? What is the gospel of peace? This means that as I stand, I am prepared to witness salvation to others. That is what the gospel of peace is all about, being at peace with God.

Luke 2:10-14 And the angel said unto them, Fear not: for, behold, I bring you good tidings of great joy, which shall be to all people.11 For unto you is born this day in the city of David a Saviour, which is Christ the Lord.12 And this shall be a sign unto you; Ye shall find the babe wrapped in swaddling clothes, lying in a manger.13 And suddenly there was with the angel a multitude of the heavenly host praising God, and saying,14 Glory to God in the highest, and on earth peace, good will toward men.

Most people, Christians included, think of God as someone who is upset with them. This is why when something bad happens on the earth, or even in our lives, we blame God, because we think He is mad with us. We must understand that because of what Jesus Christ did on the cross, we have peace with God. God is not angry with us because He satisfied His wrath on Jesus Christ on the cross.

Rom 5:1 Therefore being justified by faith, we have peace with God through our Lord Jesus Christ.

Wow! This is good news and this is why it is called the gospel—"news nearly too good to be true." Thank God for Jesus.

My Faith Shield

The Holy Spirit now gives us what He refers to as "above all": *"Above all, taking the shield of faith, wherewith ye shall be able to quench all the fiery darts of the wicked."* Faith is our most important defense. As a Christian, we use faith for everything and, without it, we are nothing. Our faith should be seen by others.

Matt 9:2 And, behold, they brought to him a man sick of the palsy, lying on a bed: and Jesus seeing their faith said unto the sick of the palsy; Son, be of good cheer; thy sins be forgiven thee.

Faith is to the kingdom of God system as money is to the world's system. Just like money answers all things in the world system, so faith answers all things in the kingdom of God system. The Christian uses faith for everything; faith is used to live by:

Rom 1:17 For therein is the righteousness of God revealed from faith to faith: as it is written, The just shall live by faith.

We are justified by faith:

Rom 3:28 Therefore we conclude that a man is justified by faith without the deeds of the law.

We walk by faith

2 Cor 5:7 *For we walk by faith, not by sight.*

Although faith is very useful in all areas of our Christian life, the Holy Spirit tells us in Eph.6:16 to use it as a shield. The purpose of a shield is to protect you from something. Note what the text said: *"Ye shall be able to quench all the fiery darts of the wicked."* This lets us know that we will not be able to stop the fiery darts of the wicked with faith, but we will be able to quench them. How does this help you?

Suppose the enemy attacks you in the area of your finances. He might use all kinds of weapons to do this such as your job, unexpected auto repairs, unexpected home repairs, etc. These are fiery darts and you use your faith to quench them. The way that we quench them is by putting our faith in the Word of God:

Isa 54:17 *No weapon that is formed against thee shall prosper; and every tongue that shall rise against thee in judgment thou shalt condemn. This is the heritage of the servants of the Lord, and their righteousness is of me, saith the Lord.*

Even though these weapons are formed against you, you know because of what the Word of God said that they will not prosper, and that takes the fire out of the dart.

I believe we all can agree that the head is the most important part of the body; we could possibly lose other parts of our body and live, but not the head. For this reason, the Holy Spirit calls us to wear *"the helmet of salvation."* Salvation is the most important thing we can ever have. To give your life to Christ and to accept Him as your personal savior is just wisdom.

Ps 111:10 *The fear of the Lord is the beginning of wisdom: a good understanding have all they that do his commandments: his praise endureth for ever.*

Understanding why the enemy attacks us will show us why salvation is so critical and how it helps us to stand.

John 10:10 *The thief cometh not, but for to steal, and to kill, and to destroy: I am come that they might have life, and that they might have it more abundantly.*

The enemy is trying to kill, steal, and destroy you. Before we can do anything for God, we must be ready to die. One of my favorite sayings is, "You are not ready to live until you are ready to die." The Bible says it like this:

Phil 1:21 *For to me to live is Christ, and to die is gain.*

2 Cor 5:8 *We are confident, I say, and willing rather to be absent from the body, and to be present with the Lord.*

If you get on a plane, one of the first things they do is prepare you in case the plane crashes. If you go into the military, the first thing they do is assign your dependant a death benefit in case you get killed. All these things are good and right, and it seems even more right that I should prepare for where I am going to spend eternity.

The Bible continues to tell us in Eph 6:17 that we should be armed with *"the sword of the Spirit, which is the word of God."* The Word of God is the only offensive weapon that we have or need because God's Word is already settled in heaven.

Ps 119:89 For ever, O Lord, thy word is settled in heaven.

We must learn to speak God's Word at all times, especially when we are under attack. We simply say what the Word of God says because we know that God honors His Word. One of the biggest struggles that the Christian may have is not that they are unable to receive from God. The struggle of the Christian will be holding on to what God has done for them. We must realize that we have an enemy and that it is not just a one-time fight; the fight continues. Satan is not going to try to overthrow you and then leave you alone. He will be back.

Luke 4:13 And when the devil had ended all the temptation, he departed from him for a season.

This text said the devil left Jesus for a season, which means he would be back. The Holy Spirit helps us with this in Eph 6:18:

Eph 6:18 Praying always with all prayer and supplication in the Spirit, and watching thereunto with all perseverance and supplication for all saints.

We must continue to pray, even after we are victorious. The Holy Spirit said, *"praying always,"* meaning I must keep my focus and attention on God always. The Holy Spirit then tells us that our prayer is with *"supplication in the Spirit."* Supplication means *"need."* Look at how the Bible puts this. Because I am a spiritual being and I am fighting a spiritual battle, things happen in the spirit before they manifest in the physical. Because of this truth, the Holy Spirit said that if I pray for the need in the Spirit and realize that the need is already met in the Spirit, then when the need manifests in the physical, likewise the solution will also manifest.

The Holy Spirit in Eph 6:18 continue and tell us to pray. Then He tells us how to pray, and what to pray for. The Holy Spirit goes on and tells us where to target our prayers. Also in Eph 6:18, the Holy Spirit tells us what to do when our answered prayer is manifested.

I Pray for You: You Pray For Me

Eph 6:18 *Praying always with all prayer and supplication in the Spirit, and watching thereunto with all perseverance and supplication for all saints.*

The important part in Eph 6: 18b is *"for all saints."* The Spirit encourages us to watch out for each other. We are to watch for the needs of all the saints. This means that I cannot aide the enemy. If I do, I am committing high treason. Watching out for each other is a very important skill of fighting a war. Our military solders are taught to watch out for each other. This is also what Jesus taught his disciples:

John 13:35 *By this shall all men know that ye are my disciples, if ye have love one to another.*

If I had to pick one characteristic that a go-ahead man must have I would say love. In fact, love is the Christian's identification card; it is how we identify ourselves to all men. Love is how we get our faith to work.

Gal 5:6 *For in Jesus Christ neither circumcision availeth anything, nor uncircumcision; but faith which worketh by love.*

Scriptures Chapter XI

Eph 6:10-18 *Finally, my brethren, be strong in the Lord, and in the power of his might.11 Put on the whole armour of God, that ye may be able to stand against the wiles of the devil.12 For we wrestle not against flesh and blood, but against principalities, against powers, against the rulers of the darkness of this world, against spiritual wickedness in high places.13 Wherefore take unto you the whole armour of God, that ye may be able to withstand in the evil day, and having done all, to stand.14 Stand therefore, having your loins girt about with truth, and having on the breastplate of righteousness;15 And your feet shod with the preparation of the gospel of peace;16 Above all, taking the shield of faith, wherewith ye shall be able to quench all the fiery darts of the wicked.17 And take the helmet of salvation, and the sword of the Spirit, which is the word of God:18 Praying always with all prayer and supplication in the Spirit, and watching thereunto with all perseverance and supplication for all saints.*

Revelation 12:10 *And I heard a loud voice saying in heaven, Now is come salvation, and strength, and the kingdom of our God, and the power of his Christ: for the accuser of our brethren is cast down, which accused them before our God day and night.*

John 6:63 *It is the spirit that quickeneth; the flesh profiteth nothing: the words that I speak unto you, they are spirit, and they are life.*

John 8:44 *Ye are of your father the devil, and the lusts of your father ye will do. He was a murderer from the beginning, and abode not in the truth, because there is no truth in him. When he speaketh a lie, he speaketh of his own: for he is a liar, and the father of it.*

1 Tim 2:1-2 *I exhort therefore, that, first of all, supplications, prayers, intercessions, and giving of thanks, be made for all men;2 For kings, and for all that are in authority; that we may lead a quiet and peaceable life in all godliness and honesty.*

1 Cor 15:57-58 *But thanks be to God, which giveth us the victory through our Lord Jesus Christ.58 Therefore, my beloved brethren, be ye stedfast, unmoveable, always abounding in the work of the Lord, forasmuch as ye know that your labour is not in vain in the Lord.*

Rom 3:21-24 *But now the righteousness of God without the law is manifested, being witnessed by the law and the prophets;22 Even the righteousness of God which is by faith of Jesus Christ unto all and upon all them that believe: for there is no difference:23 For all have sinned, and come short of the glory of God.*

Luke 2:10-14 *And the angel said unto them, Fear not: for, behold, I bring you good tidings of great joy, which shall be to all people.11 For unto you is born this day in the city of David a Saviour, which is Christ the Lord.12 And this shall be a sign unto you; Ye shall find the babe wrapped in swaddling clothes, lying in a manger.13 And suddenly there was with the angel a multitude of the heavenly host praising God, and saying,14 Glory to God in the highest, and on earth peace, good will toward men.*

Rom 5:1 *Therefore being justified by faith, we have peace with God through our Lord Jesus Christ.*

Matt 9:2 *And, behold, they brought to him a man sick of the palsy, lying on a bed: and Jesus seeing their faith said unto the sick of the palsy; Son, be of good cheer; thy sins be forgiven thee.*

Rom 1:17 *For therein is the righteousness of God revealed from faith to faith: as it is written, The just shall live by faith.*

Rom 3:28 *Therefore we conclude that a man is justified by faith without the deeds of the law.*

2 Cor 5:7 *For we walk by faith, not by sight.*

Isa 54:17 *No weapon that is formed against thee shall prosper; and every tongue that shall rise against thee in judgment thou shalt condemn. This is the heritage of the servants of the Lord, and their righteousness is of me, saith the Lord.*

Ps 111:10 *The fear of the Lord is the beginning of wisdom: a good understanding have all they that do his commandments: his praise endureth for ever.*

John 10:10 *The thief cometh not, but for to steal, and to kill, and to destroy: I am come that they might have life, and that they might have it more abundantly.*

Phil 1:21 *For to me to live is Christ, and to die is gain.*

2 Cor 5:8 *We are confident, I say, and willing rather to be absent from the body, and to be present with the Lord.*

Ps 119:89 *For ever, O Lord, thy word is settled in heaven.*

Luke 4:13 *And when the devil had ended all the temptation, he departed from him for a season.*

John 13:35 *By this shall all men know that ye are my disciples, if ye have love one to another.*

Gal 5:6 *For in Jesus Christ neither circumcision availeth anything, nor uncircumcision; but faith which worketh by love.*

CHAPTER XII

BEING A GO-AHEAD MAN

Being a go-ahead man is simply being a man of God. It is being the man that God called you to be, walking in the will of God for your life. One might say, "When I discover God's will for my life, I believe I can do it." That is a good attitude to have, but once you discover God's will for your life, you will need God to bring it to pass. We must learn to do things God's way:

Rom 12:2 And be not conformed to this world: but be ye transformed by the renewing of your mind, that ye may prove what is that good, and acceptable, and perfect, will of God.

We cannot even begin to know God's will for our lives until we change the way we think. We must understand that the world's way of thinking is going to try to influence us on every side, but we must not conform to it. In Rom 12:2 the word "prove" is *"δοκιμαζω"* in the Greek, and it is pronounced "dokimazo," which means: *"to approve, allow, discern, examine."* This means that God wants me to approve of the plan that He has for my life, and He tells me how to do it. By renewing my mind to

128

God's way of thinking, I will begin to see things like God sees them. When I see thing like God sees them, and then I can come into agreement with what God's will is for my life. We must learn to think like God thinks. This is what renewing the mind is about; I must think with the mind of Christ.

The go-ahead man must learn to keep God's laws and His precepts. He must never forget that God created everything, and He knows how He intended for it to work. Every born-again believer is a servant of God; therefore, they must learn to follow His instructions and do things His way. Christ is our example; we must follow His lead and take the roads He tells us to take. One of my favorite saying is "you can't go down the wrong road and end up in the right place."

Prov 14:12 *There is a way which seemeth right unto a man, but the end thereof are the ways of death.*

Notice the text said, *"there is a way."* From this we understand that there is one right way and one wrong way, but each way leads to other ways. In order for us to end right, we must begin right. The Holy Spirit must be the guide in our decisions. This is the answer to the age-old question, "Why do bad things happen to good people?", because good people make bad decisions. But halleluiah, we serve a good God and no matter how far off the path we have gotten; we are only one decision away from getting back on track.

The institution of marriage is the first institution that God formed. In God's eyes, how you get along with your spouse is more important than how you get along with your fellow church members. God is all about family. God knows what it takes to make the family work; after all, look at all the children He has. When God called me into the ministry, the first thing He taught me was that my first ministry was to my wife and then to my family, in that order. God knows how important the go-ahead man's wife is to him, and He also knows that behind every go-ahead man is a go-ahead woman.

Mom & Dad, Look What I Found!

Prov 18:22 Whoso findeth a wife findeth a good thing, and obtaineth favour of the Lord.

This stricture helps us understand that the wife is a wife before the man finds her. In most cases, the reason we find something is because we are looking for it. Another important thing to realize here is that the man is supposed to find the woman, not the other way around. Notice also the Scripture calls the wife *"a good thing."* What would you consider a good thing?

According to Strong's Number 2896, "a good thing" means *"benefit, prosperity, happiness, and moral good."* I find it interesting that the word beauty does not appear in the definition. God did not make us part of his church based on how we looked.

One of the biggest mistakes that couples make is to get married thinking they are going to change each other. The man must realize that he cannot marry a woman with the intent of making her a wife; that's going down the wrong road. God makes the woman a wife, and God gives her favor. The text said that whoever finds her will obtain favor from the

Lord. What is this favor? Simply put, the favor is the wife that he finds. It is as though God makes something that is good, attaches favor to it, and then hides it. God wants you to find your wife. God even gives us guidelines to go by, and tell us things that we should be looking for in a wife, but we must make the final decision.

Some may think that there are certain people that God has created to be together. Personally, I cannot find where the Bible teaches that. The only couple that God created to be together in the Bible was Adam and Eve, and they still fell short. Adam is the only man who could ever truly say:

Gen 3:12 *And the man said, The woman whom thou gavest to be with me, she gave me of the tree, and I did eat.*

To the go-ahead man, divorce is not an option. The go-ahead man understands that he is in a covenant with his wife and it is till death. The go-ahead man not only has a covenant with his wife, but it was also witnessed by God. Can you imagine if we were still under the Old Covenant and the only legal way to break a blood covenant was through death? If the man or woman wanted a divorce, they were simply just killed. I bet then we would figure out a way to resolve our issues. As a go-ahead man you never look for ways to get out of the marriage, but you look for ways to make it work. We need only to think about the goodness that God has shown us and the patience God has with us and we will realize that to really change things we must show love and kindness.

Jer 31:3 *The Lord hath appeared of old unto me, saying, Yea, I have loved thee with an everlasting love: therefore with lovingkindness have I drawn thee.*

SCRIPTURES CHAPTER XII

Rom 12:2 *And be not conformed to this world: but be ye transformed by the renewing of your mind, that ye may prove what is that good, and acceptable, and perfect, will of God.*

Prov 14:12 *There is a way which seemeth right unto a man, but the end thereof are the ways of death.*

Prov 18:22 *Whoso findeth a wife findeth a good thing, and obtaineth favour of the Lord.*

Gen 3:12 *And the man said, The woman whom thou gavest to be with me, she gave me of the tree, and I did eat.*

Jer 31:3 *The Lord hath appeared of old unto me, saying, Yea, I have loved thee with an everlasting love: therefore with lovingkindness have I drawn thee.*

Printed in the United States
By Bookmasters